The Flower Garden in England

Richard Gorer

B. T BATSFORD LTD
London and Sydney

First published 1975
Copyright © Richard Gorer, 1975

ISBN 0 7134 2858 9

Printed and bound by Cox and Wyman Ltd,
London, Fakenham and Reading
for the publishers
B. T. Batsford Ltd, 4 Fitzhardinge Street, London W1H 0AH
and
23 Cross Street, Brookvale, NSW 2100, Australia

Contents

The Illustrations

Acknowledgements

Illustration 1 is reproduced by arrangement with the Radio
Times Hulton Picture Library; is by courtesy of Sotheby & Co.
Illustrations 20, 22 and 24 are reproduced by arrangement with
Kenneth Scowen, numbers 25 and 26 by arrangement with A. F.
Kersting. Numbers 8, 9b, 10 11, 12 and 13 are from the *Gardener's
Magazine* of 1839, 9a from the *Gardener's Magazine* of 1830;
14 and 18 are from *Floral World* 1868, 15 from the same maga-
zine for 1866. Number 16 is taken from *Formal Gardens in
England & Scotland* by H. Inigo Triggs, 1902; 17 is from *Rustic
Adornments for Homes of Taste*, Shirley Hibberd, 1870; 19 is
from *My Garden*, Alfred Smee, 1872, and 23 from the *Gardener's
Chronicle*, 1899. Nos 2, 4, 5 and 21 are from the publisher's
collection.

Preface

ALTHOUGH this is, so far as my knowledge goes, a pioneer work on this particular subject, no work dealing with garden history can fail to acknowledge a debt to the writings of Miles Hadfield, which I have used extensively.

I must also acknowledge debts of gratitude to Mr John Harvey, not only for his valuable *Early Gardening Catalogues*, but also for an amount of information conveyed in correspondence and also to Mr. Peter Hunt, for many valuable suggestions and also for the loan of some early gardening magazines.

Stelling Church, September 1974

I

Introduction

THE FLOWER GARDEN with its beds and borders, its rockeries, pools and shrubberies seems so much a part of a long tradition that it is rather deflating to find that, according to garden historians, it is barely 150 years old. Before about 1830, although flowers were grown fairly extensively, it would appear that they were mainly grown for decorating the house. One walked round the garden to admire the prospect, but no one seems to have suggested that growing flowers were among the features that would call for admiration. Trees were certainly desirable, and clumps of shrubs were often highly thought of, but flowers, so far as most of the available literature can inform us, were relegated to a small enclosure where the lady of the house might divert herself but which the impressionable visitor would be hurried past.

The reason for this is assumed to be the paucity of material that was available until the plant collectors brought back the fruits of other continents, but I am not sure that this argument is altogether valid. Think of the normal contents of the herbaceous border, a feature that is now vanishing. There are lupins, delphiniums, Michaelmas daisies, pyrethrums, thalictrums, geraniums, irises, bergamot. The only relatively modern introductions are the pyrethrum, which arrived in 1804, and the lupin which was not received until 1826, although the tree lupin had been available since 1793 and *L. nootkatensis* had arrived in 1794. Admittedly the nineteenth century saw the largest number of plant introductions of any and, as we shall see, the type of plants introduced affected the design of gardens to a considerable degree; but to assume from that fact that flower gardens were more or less ignored before, say, the introductions of Douglas is, I venture to think, fallacious.

The literature of gardens has tended to concentrate on the great and magnificent, while the English flower garden is small and intimate. If you only have a few acres you do not call in William Kent or Capability Brown to landscape the garden; you only do that when you number your acres in hundreds and if you have this large acreage you must design on a massive, somewhat public, scale. Five acres can be intimate, but five hundred cannot. Not until Loudon wrote *The Suburban Gardener* in 1838 was there any written acknowledgement that a garden was not necessarily a vast demesne. It was not, with a few exceptions, until the nineteenth century that text-books appeared on growing plants.

There is, however, a more lowly branch of literature which may make us revise our opinions slightly and this is the catalogues issued by nurserymen. If people were able to make a living out of growing and selling plants, then it is reasonable to assume that a large number of people must have wished to purchase them. And if they purchased plants, then they must have grown them in gardens. If we extrapolate from commercial considerations a rather different picture emerges of gardening activity in the late seventeenth and eighteenth centuries, which suggests that our feeling that the English flower garden is a long-established tradition may be more accurate than the normal published references would suggest.

There is a long tradition in England of great plantsmen – people who obtained and grew very many more plants than the general run of gardeners, starting with Nicholas Lete, that 'worthy merchant' whom both Gerard and Parkinson mention, through the Tradescants, Evelyn, Sherburn, Miller, Collinson, Fothergill, Hibbert and Lambert, while pre-eminent among these is the actual, though not the titular founder of Kew Gardens, Sir Joseph Banks. It is to these men and people like them, whose names are now lost, that the English flower garden owes its adventurous quality.

However, it must be borne in mind that the plantsman is not

necessarily a good gardener from the point of view of arranging and grouping plants. His object is to grow plants that have not been grown before. There is no reason why his garden should not also be agreeable to see – it seems likely that Peter Collinson's garden at Mill Hill was delightful to look at as well as being full of fascinating plants – but this need not necessarily have been the case with everyone. As we shall see, the catalogue of the Tradescants' garden at Lambeth contains a large number of plants now regarded as weeds. The Tradescants seem to have thought their collection of nettles as interesting as their collection of cyclamens, and many of the plantsmen's gardens may well have been private botanic gardens rather than flower gardens in the sense that we use the term. Even as late as the beginning of this century we find that remarkable plantsman, the Rev. Henry Ewbank, saying that his garden, although full of remarkable plants, was 'not at all pretty', and one could certainly find contemporary examples of the same tendency. By and large the successful flower gardener will let the plantsman do the exploratory work and then adopt his most satisfactory introductions into his own designs. To take a recent example, a large number of *Meconopsis* species have been introduced to Britain in this century but only *M. betonicifolia* has become a popular plant. The others remaining in cultivation (some, such as the scarlet *M. punicea*, have been lost) are found only in the gardens of specialists.

Social attitudes should not be neglected, and I have wondered if the very austere selection of trees employed by Capability Brown (elm, oak, beech, lime, plane, scots pine, larch and, for special effects, cedar) had anything to do with his clients' being aristocrats. Were flowers perhaps regarded as being rather bourgeois and middle-class? After all, the horse chestnut had been in cultivation in England since 1629 and one might have thought that its flowers would have given it some additional attractions, but generally the great garden landscapists seem to have avoided it. Not everyone was as austere as Brown, but there seems to have been a general feeling that when planning a landscape flowers might well be an intrusion. We now know that this is not so. The rhododendrons and hydrangeas at Stourhead may be both historically incorrect and artistically wrong, yet they do nothing to spoil the original conception. At Sheffield Park there are probably very few plants left of Brown's original design, yet the effect is still entrancing. It would seem that if your basic framework is right, the intrusion of minor alien elements, which is what flowers are in these circumstances, will do no harm at all.

Throughout the years, garden design has fluctuated between the formal and symmetrical and the informal and asymmetric (or with the symmetry carefully disguised). Rather oddly, the formal, geometric garden is the more primitive of the two styles; but perhaps this is not so strange. Horace's precept that there is an art in concealing artifice (if that is what *ars celare artem* means) must have appeared rather sophisticated, and the large formal garden must have been easier to conceive than the wilder landscapes of the English school. It is an amusing example of the general ignorance that exists on these subjects that William Morris was horrified by Victorian carpet bedding, when it was, in reality, a return to the style of his beloved Mediaeval times. The Tudor knot garden would have been greatly enriched if amaranthus and alternantheras had been known in those days. As it was, they tended to fill their geometric beds with coloured soil or coloured pebbles, a phenomenon that also turned up again in the later part of the nineteenth century.

Bacon very rightly noted that people created great houses before they created gardens. The idea of flowers for ornament seems to be quite a late idea in western Europe, although it had existed in China for at least a thousand years and, presumably, for some considerable time in the Near East. However, in the general neglect of flowers there were two exceptions, suitably enough depicted in the Knossos frescoes, namely the rose and the lily, and these seem to have been used as adjuncts of religious ceremonies since time immemorial. Their popularity may be gauged to a large extent by the way that quite other flowers are described with rose or lily in their names. Such plants as primrose, rose of Sharon, rock rose, lily-of-the-valley, arum lily, St Bruno's lily, trout lily – all bear witness to the extreme popularity of these two flowers. The only attribute the rose and the lily seem to have in common is fragrance, and sweet scent in flowers was obviously relished at a time when neither soap, sewage disposal nor running water was available and unpleasing scents must have been the rule, not the exception.

The affection for the white *Lilium candidum* is easy enough to understand: it is showy, has an air of great purity and a very heavy perfume. The reason for the rose's popularity is less easy to comprehend. Although Herodotus mentions a rose with 30 petals, the majority of roses in Greek and Roman times must have been single and so the flowers would prove short-lived. The perfume is attractive, but not particularly strong in most species. Although the reasons for the rose's popularity seem somewhat hard to define, the fact remains that these two flowers were grown for ornament at a time when other flowers were grown solely for their medical uses. It was, of course, the monasteries that had most of these herbal gardens and, even today, the presence of *Paeonia mascula* in the wild, outside its native locality of central France, is almost certainly an indication that at one time there was a monastery in the immediate environs. It even appears in *The British Flora*, as it survives on the island of Steep Holme, and has also turned up in such unlikely places as Cyprus and Russia. But the monastery garden, although it might contain many plants that we now grow for their flowers, was purely functional. Plants were grown either for food or for their medical virtues.

In Roman times, gardens contained features such as topiary and fountains, and when the Renaissance came the Roman garden was reproduced on more grandiose terms. However, Italy is hot and dry in the summer and the two most desired attributes of a garden would have been shade and water, ingredients of which the English are liable to have too much. The great Renaissance gardens could have had little message for us. Later, the French adapted the Renaissance garden to their cooler climate, and it may be that the early English gardens were influenced by the French. In any case they tended to consist of a parterre near the house, which could well be ornamented by geometric beds, called knots or trails, while beyond there would be walks, closely bordered with hedges that might well be trained behind ornamental trellis-work. If you were rich and ostentatious you might make a maze or a labyrinth. There would be lawns, there might well be ponds and fountains, there was almost certainly a huge mound, dating from the time when it was necessary to see over the battlements, and which still persisted although its *raison d'être* had vanished. Statues, summer houses, temples might occur, but flowers would be scarce.

The knots would be bordered with different plants, of which, according to Parkinson, the most favoured were thrift, germander, box, marjoram, savory, thyme and santolina. This latter plant, however, was apparently a fairly recent introduction of 1629 and was, presumably, not available to Tudor gardeners. Germander is not an easy plant to identify. The name is used for most species of *Teucrium* and Parkinson depicts two plants, one of which is *T. fruticans* while the other is not easily recognised. Parkinson says the one used for edging will grow thick and 'may be kept in some form and proportion with cutting'. Moreover, the 'cuttings are much used as a strawing herb for houses, being pretty and sweet'. A plant that can be cut seems to exclude the small *Teucrium chamaedrys*, which is naturalised in England and so might be thought to have been introduced from gardens. The most likely candidate would seem to be the grey-leaved *T. polium*. According to Philip Miller, this is a most useful plant with 'a piercing grateful scent, so quick as to cause sneezing'. It is not, however, reliably hardy except 'in a dry soil and a warm situation . . . but in very hard winters they are frequently killed if they are not protected by mats or some other covering'. This was also, apparently, one of those few plants to which cats are much attracted; 'where there is a great number of plants together, the cats seldom touch them'. Marjoram seems a rather odd plant to find in this list as it is not evergreen, but presumably its fragrant leaves were thought to compensate for this. Obviously what was looked for was a low-growing evergreen that would remain compact.

Parkinson mentions that some people used rooted cuttings of yew and juniper, but points out that they will 'soon grow too great and stubbed, and force you to take up your knot sooner than if it were planted with Box', which Parkinson thinks is easily the best edging.

The embroidered parterre need not necessarily have had even plants to define the edges of the beds. Parkinson points out that you could have dead materials, such as lead, boards, bones, tiles,

1 *Le Livre de Rusticon:* a probably idealised fifteenth-century garden

2 Amport Hall: a modern Tudor Knot Garden with patterns in clipped box and many of the interstices filled with coloured earths

3 Brueghel's 'Spring': a country garden in the sixteenth century

4 Delahaye Place: Bacon's idea of flowers in front of fruit trees

etc., so the Tudor knot garden could have been completely without living plants. By the close of the Elizabethan age the garden had been, if not completely transformed, considerably altered.

One point should perhaps be made. All gardens are subject to alteration as tastes change and as plants grow, but the flower garden is the least permanent of all. The topiary at Levens Hall has been kept going since the end of the seventeenth century. Although much of the work of Brown and Repton has been altered, enough remains for us to appreciate their design, but the famous flower gardens of the eighteenth century at Mill Hill and East Ham have quite vanished, although some of the trees that were planted at the same time still survive. Moreover, old paintings do not help us much. We do not know how typical or unusual are the flower gardens shown in old paintings, although it is from these that we must take our impressions. It is easy enough to find out what people grew, but until the nineteenth century it is not easy to find out how they grew them.

It is not clear whether all the early northern European gardens were the same, but in *Le Livre de Rusticon* there is a miniature of a fifteenth-century garden. This shows a background of ornamental trellis-work, behind which is woodland. In the background is what looks suspiciously like a rockery on which some plants have been placed. In the foreground are shaped beds, with tapestry-like patterns, presumably edged with some plants, but this is by no means clear. The beds themselves seem to be edged with a stone coping and within this edging is a row of unidentifiable plants in full flower, while rather larger plants are in the centre of the beds. In addition there are a number of plants in tubs – possibly oranges although they look too small – and other flowering plants in stone vases. Since one of these looks like a *Miltonia*, it would seem probable that this is a somewhat idealised scene. The potted plants are being inspected by an important-looking functionary who is presumably giving directions about where they should be placed. Anyway, the garden is quite flowery, although I suppose that the flowers that edge the beds might only be the thrift.

When we come to the sixteenth century, some information can be obtained from Brueghel's 'Spring'. In this we see part of an elaborate parterre, with the beds raised and edged by tiles or boards, while an immense labour force is cleaning everything up. Evidently they were quite bare during the winter. There are a large number of potted plants and trees being brought out, many of them clipped into various shapes and these are about to be put in the centres of the beds. Some of the beds are having seeds cast on them, while others are being edged with plants, although it is not clear whether these are flowers, herbs or vegetables. Since the parterre abuts on the farmyard it is not easy to distinguish the useful from the ornamental. In the foreground some people are digging away at what would appear to be a border in which one or two plants are seen, but these may well be weeds, as they appear in the portion that awaits digging. It certainly looks as though the beds of the parterre are going to have centres of specimen trees and flowers underneath them. Still there are many unanswered questions. Where, for example, was the topiary work over-wintered? What were the seeds that were being sown? The *Livre de Rusticon* is somewhat idealised, but this looks like straightforward reporting. And what happened to the vines being trained up an arched, trellised arbour? It is all rather different from what we might expect from reports of the grander gardens of the period.

───2───

The Elizabethan and Jacobaean Garden
The First Influx of Exotics

qr By the end of the sixteenth and the beginning of the
𝕏 seventeenth century we are on slightly firmer ground. This
period coincides with many plant introductions and (as always
apparently) the introduction of large numbers of new plants had
an effect on garden design that might not always have been
foreseen.

Although Bacon's essay *Of Gardens* was not published until
1625, many of his other essays had been published in 1597 and
they may all date from around that period. From Bacon's essay
we get some idea of what the Elizabethan flower garden may
have been like. He opens with a catalogue of plants that will
beautify every month. 'For December and January and the latter
part of November, you must take such things as are green all
winter: holly; ivy; bays; juniper; cypress trees; yew; pine-apple
trees; fir trees; rosemary; lavender; periwinkle, the white, the
purple and the blue; germander; flags; orange trees, lemon trees
and myrtles, if they be stoved; and sweet marjoram, warm set.'
I cannot think what pine-apples trees can have been, unless it
were the Norway spruce (*Picea abies*) which sometimes has what
are referred to as pine-apple galls, it could also be *Pinus pinea*.
Cypress trees are presumably cypresses, but they are not very
hardy. Presumably the orange, lemon and myrtle were trundled
indoors during the winter, in which case they would not have
been of much advantage for winter decoration in the garden.
The reference to the herbaceous sweet marjoram is presumably
a mistake. As we shall see, Bacon was not a very knowledgeable

gardener, although doubtless enthusiastic. Incidentally, although some of his flowering seasons appear fantastic (and are) we should remember that he was writing before the reform of the calendar and so January 1st then was today's January 12th. Thus for 'the latter part of January and February' he mentions the mezereon tree, yellow and grey crocuses, primroses, anemones, early tulips, *Hyacinthus orientalis, Chamaeiris* and *Fritillaria*. This is evidently only partly accurate. *Daphne mezereum*, crocus and perhaps some anemones would be all that would usually flower at this period.

'For March there come violets, specially the single blue, which are the earliest; the yellow daffodil; the daisy; the almond tree in blossom; the peach tree in blossom; the cornelian tree in blossom; sweet briar.' This last must evidently be a mistake, unless he means that the leaves will start to unfurl or unless sweet briar meant something different from what it does now. The cornelian tree (*Cornus mas*) should have been in the February list.

'In April follow the double white violet; the wall-flower; the stock-gillyflower; the cowslip; the fleur-de-luce and lilies of all natures; rosemary flowers; the tulipa; the double peony; the pale daffodil; the French honeysuckle; the cherry tree in blossom; the damson and plum trees in blossom; the white-thorn [White-beam] in leaf; the lilac tree.' We will forgive him a lot for indicating the emerging leaves of the whitebeam as an ornament, but lilies of all descriptions in April sound unlikely, although he is probably thinking of Crown Imperials. The 'pale daffodil' could be an asphodel or *Narcissus poeticus*. April sounds a little early for Stock and if the French honeysuckle is *Hedysarum coronarium*, which is known by that name today, April is far too early.

'In May and June come pinks of all sorts, specially the blush pink; roses of all kinds, except the musk, which comes later; honeysuckles; strawberries; bugloss; columbine; the French marigold; flos Africanus; cherry tree in fruit; ribes; figs in fruit; rasps; vine flowers; lavender in flower; the sweet satyrium with the white flower; herba muscaria; lilium convallium; the apple tree in blossom.' This is quite a list. Flos Africanus was the African marigold; the sweet satyrium with the white flower must have been *Platanthera bifolia,* an unexpected garden plant at that time. Herba muscaria was presumably *Muscari plumosus,* although other muscari were around at the time they tend to flower earlier; this, however, means little with Bacon as we have seen. Lilium convallium is lily-of-the-valley.

'In July come gillyflowers of all varieties; musk-roses; the lime tree in blossom; early pears and plums in fruit; ginnitings; codlins.' Gillyflowers will mean carnations here. Ginnitings were the first apples to ripen; the name may be a corruption of June-eating which, as Jeneton, survived as late as 1920 and may still be in some orchards.

'In August come plums of all sorts in fruit; pears, apricots; barberries; filberts; musk-melons; monkshoods of all colours.' It will be noted that Bacon is running out of flowering plants and this was a great problem for the early flower gardener.

'In September come grapes, apples, poppies of all colours, peaches, melocotones, nectarines, cornelians, wardens, quinces.' Wardens were cooking pears. September seems to be rather late for poppies.

'In October and the beginning of November come services, medlars, bullaces, roses cut or removed to come late, hollyhocks and such like.' The plans for late roses are interesting. Presumably they were pruned back hard in the spring and produced only a few flowers in the autumn. Why moving the bushes would have that result is rather unclear and it was probably an unreliable method of obtaining late flowers. It seems very late for hollyhocks, but Bacon is not a reliable guide to times of flowering.

It will be remembered that Bacon was very insistent on growing plants that would perfume the air, Thus 'Roses, damask and red, are fast flowers of their smells; so that you may walk a whole row of them and find nothing of their sweetness; yea though it be in a morning's dew.' Similarly bay and rosemary are unsatisfactory.

'That which above all other yields the sweetest smell in the air is the violet; specially the white double violet which comes twice a year, about the middle of April and about Bartholomew-tide.' Among other recommended perfumers is 'strawberry leaves dying, which yield a most excellent cordial smell'. I think this should probably read 'strawberry leaves drying', which are more liable to give a perfume, i.e. strawberry leaves in hot weather.

'But those which perfume the air most delightfully, not passed by as the rest, but being trodden upon and crushed, are three: that is burnet, wild thyme and water-mints. Therefore you are to set whole alleys with them, to have the pleasure when you walk or tread.' The Elizabethans and Jacobaeans wrote fine sonorous prose, but it is rather convoluted. How can you walk without treading?

Having decided what he is going to grow, Bacon now turns to the actual design of the garden which he thinks should ideally be of 30 acres. This is divided into a 4-acre lawn in front of the house, while on either side is a walk with hedges 12 ft. high, shaped by trellis, or, since for some inexplicable reason most garden design terms like ballet steps are couched in French, perhaps we should say *treillage*. These trellises were quite elaborate and served as a sort of template for trimming the hedges. These particular allies that Bacon recommended were to be covered, so that the trellis was presumably to be shaped like a tunnel. Bacon was firm about not having the part of the lawn nearest the house arranged in a geometrical knot-garden. 'They be but toys,' he observes 'you may see as good sights many times in tarts.'

Beyond the lawn was the main garden, comprising 12 acres, while on either side of these 12 acres were compartments of 4 acres each. The main garden was 'encompassed on all the four sides with a stately arched hedge'. This hedge was exceedingly elaborate. The arches were placed on pillars of carpenter's work (presumably trellis again) 10 ft. high and 6 across and extending for 4 ft. above the apex of the arch, which was also framed by trellis. There was 6 ft. between the arches. Over each arch was 'a little turret with a belly, enough to receive a cage of birds, and over every space between the arches some other little figure, with broad plates of round coloured glass, gilt, for the sun to play upon. But this hedge I intend to be raised upon a bank, not steep, but gently sloped, of some six foot, set all with flowers.' A 10 ft. hedge would have taken some years to grow, and one wonders what it looked like before it were completed and how on earth did they manage to get up and feed the birds? However, from our point of view the interesting part is the sloping beds at the foot of the hedge where the flowers were. Although the hedge is said to encompass the whole of the main garden, Bacon later modifies this to say that there must be no allies with hedges at either end of the enclosure, so as not to interfere with the view from the lawn to the main garden and from the main garden to the heath.

As to how this main garden is to be ornamented, Bacon is rather vague. 'I leave it to variety of device; advising, nevertheless, that whatsoever form you cast it into, first, it be not too busy or full of work. Wherein I, for my part, do not like images cut out in juniper or other garden stuff: they be for children. Little low hedges, round like welts, with some pretty pyramids I like well; and in some places, fair columns upon frames of carpenter's work.'

Flowers seem to play no part in this main garden, which appears to be entirely of topiary work. In the middle of this garden is a mount 30 ft. high, at the top of which is 'some fine banqueting house with some chimneys neatly cast, and without too much glass'. There are three ascents to this mount which is girdled by three alleys: 'enough for four to walk abreast; which I would have to be perfect circles without any bulwarks or embossments'. Also in the main garden there are 'some fair alleys, ranged on both sides with fruit trees, and some pretty tufts of fruit trees' as well as 'arbours with seats, set in some decent order'. However, these must, in Bacon's eyes, be used sparingly as the main garden should give an impression of openness. If the weather is very hot and oppressive and you need shade you then repair to the two side plots. These are full of hedged alleys, so that you can be in the shade at all times if you so wish, while some will be arched over, so that 'you may walk as in a gallery'. These alleys are to be gravel, so that your feet will not get wet. They will also contain a good many fruit trees and 'the borders, wherein you plant your fruit trees, be fair and large, and low, and not steep; and set with fine flowers, but thin and sparingly lest they deceive the trees'. In other words, the flowers must not take too much nourishment from the fruit trees. The main garden may also have fountains and a bathing pool, as long as the water is always moving so that it is kept clear and clean. 'Pools mar all and make the garden unwholesome and full of flies and frogs.'

From our point of view, the most important section is the 'heath' and it is worth quoting the whole of Bacon's description. 'For the heath . . . I wish it to be framed as much as may be, to a natural wildness. Trees I would have none in it; but some thickets, made only of sweet briar and honeysuckle, and some wild vine amongst; and the ground set with violets, strawberries and primroses. For these are sweet and prosper in the shade. And these to be in the heath, here and there, not in any order. I like also little heaps in the nature of mole hills (such as are in wild heaths) to be set, some with wild thyme, some with pinks, some with germander that gives a good flower to the eye, some with periwinkle, some with violets, some with strawberries, some with cowslips, some with daisies, some with red roses, some with lilium convallium, some with sweet-williams red, some with bear's foot, and the like low flowers, being withal sweet and sightly. Part of which heaps to be with standards of little bushes pricked upon their top, and part without. The standards to be roses, juniper, holly, barberries (but here and there because of the smell of their blossoms), red currants, gooseberries, rosemary, bays, sweet-briar and such like. But these standards to be kept with cutting, that they grow not out of course.'

It would be interesting to know how much of a novelty this was. No writer about gardens, apart from Bacon, has ever suggested this particular type of wilderness-garden, although we do not really know what the bosquets or groves contained. Bacon certainly does not suggest that this is anything out of the ordinary, and it may well have been a feature of many gardens, on a less extensive scale than the six acres that Bacon recommends. I do not think we should take the mole-hills too literally. I imagine they were quite considerable mounds. One could scarcely cover a mole-hill with red roses and top it with a standard bay. Bear's foot, incidentally, is *Helleborus*, but this may be a misprint for bear's ear or *Auricula*.

To sum up, the Baconian garden had flowers in borders in front of hedges, between fruit trees and in a special garden of their own. They were certainly a feature of the garden, even if not the most prominent one.

Parkinson's *Paradisi in sole* was printed in 1629, with the subtitle 'A Garden of all Sorts of Pleasant Flowers, which our English Air will permit to be nursed up'; although he includes a few plants which are definitely tender. Most of this book is a descriptive catalogue of flowers, but he does give a few gardening hints in his introductory chapters. If possible, he advises, the house and buildings should be on the north side of the garden 'so they may be a defence of much sufficiency to safeguard it from many injurious cold nights and days, which else might spoil the pride thereof in the bud'. If you cannot supply these, or brick or stone walls he suggests 'high grown and well spread trees'. Of soils he says that black mould is easily the best, although sandy loam is nearly as good, while 'the stiff clay is the very worst'. It can, however, be improved by incorporating 'good store of chalk, lime or sand, or else ashes either of wood or of sea-coals (which is the best for this ground). He also maintains that bulbs and tubers need less manuring than herbaceous plants. Before planting the beds you should clean the soil by removing all 'annoyances . . . as stones, weeds, roots of trees, bushes, etc.'.

The shape of the garden is not important; it can be round, triangular, rectangular or square. This latter is best as it matches the house, all the back windows of which will open on it. In the garden there may be 'walks either open or close, either public or private, a maze or wilderness, a rock or mount, with a fountain in the midst thereof to convey water to every part of the garden, either in pipes under the ground, or brought by hand and emptied into large cisterns or great Turkey jars, placed in con-venient places to serve as an ease to water the nearest parts thereunto. Arbours also being both graceful and necessary may be appointed in such convenient places, as at corners, or else where, as may be most fit to serve both for shadow and rest after walking.' However you shape your knots you must leave ample space for alleys and walks, 'for the fairer and larger your allies and walks be, the more grace your Garden shall have, the less harm the herbs and flowers shall receive by passing by them that grow next unto the allies' sides, and the better shall your weeders cleanse both the beds and the allies.' The garden is composed of knots, or beds, and trails, or borders. These will be edged either with living plants or with lead, boards or other inert material. The beds themselves were planted mainly with spring flowers; Parkinson suggests 'Daffodils, Fritillarias, Hyacinths, Crocus, Lilies, Irises, Tulips, Anemones and Auriculas'.

Towards the end of the sixteenth century there had been a great influx of exotic flowers. Some the Spanish had brought from Mexico; some the French had brought in from North America, but the largest number had come from Turkey; a large number through that enterprising ambassador Ghislaine de Busbecq. It would seem that it is to him that the first glimpse of these floral riches was due and they were publicised by Clusius. Other travellers also brought plants back, and eventually trade was opened with Turkish nurserymen, who got a bad name for only sending single ranunculi when double ones had been paid for. The majority of these Turkish flowers were garden developments of local wild flowers of the Near East, but there were also a few more exotic plants from India and China, presumably brought along the Silk Road. These included such plants as *Hemerocallis fulva* and *citrina*, the day lilies and, possibly the Prince's feather (*Celosia*) and love-lies-bleeding (*Amaranthus caudatus*).

Parkinson's list starts with bulbous and tuberous subjects, then herbaceous plants and finally ornamental shrubs, although the order is not followed exactly. Lists tend to be rather tedious reading, but I think it as well to reproduce his list so far as species go, while passing over the large number of cultivars[1] of such plants as tulips and hyacinths. This will give us a fairly clear picture of what plants the early seventeenth-century gardener had to work with. Although every plant is handsomely illustrated, it is not always easy to identify them correctly and a few I have felt doubtful about.

Parkinson started off with lilies, but his first two are now classified as fritillaries so will be included with the others of this genus. The lilies were *L.L. bulbiferum, canadense, candidum, chalcedonicum, martagon* (4 cvs) *pomponium* (?) and *pyrenaicum*. Possibly we should add *L. carniolicum* to the list as the bright red martagon of Hungary. Many of these are fairly easy

---

[1] This word, abbreviated as cv, is used to denote variants from wild plants that have only occured in cultivation, whereas varieties, if the word is used correctly, occur among wild plants.

to identify, but of the 13 fritillaries many seem to be forms of *F. meleagris*. We can be fairly sure about *F.F. imperialis, persica, lusitanica* (or perhaps *hispanica*), *pyrenaica* and *tubiflora*. There is also that very strange plant with a small raceme of flowers which Miller called *F. nigra* and which Curtis thought was a form of *pyrenaica*. This does not seem to have been seen since the eighteenth century.

Parkinson depicts a huge number of tulips, mostly florists' gesnerianas, but presumably some suaveolens, which he calls praecoces. There is a mention of striped-leaved tulips, which makes one wonder if *T. greigii* was around at that time. Of species one can only recognise *T. silvestris* and something that looks like *T. cretica*.

A lot of rather odd plants come under Parkinson's narcissus category, such as *Sprekelia formosissima*, presumably brought from Mexico by the Spaniards, *Sternbergia lutea* and *Zephyranthes atamasco*, described as *Narcissus virgineus*. Of true narcissi there is an enormous selection, including not only nearly every species in cultivation at the present time, but also the autumnal flowering *N.N. serotinus, elegans* and *viridiflora* (but all the bulbs of this last one had died). There were a large number of double daffodils and the selection was very large. Also among the narcissi were *Pancratium maritimum* and *P. illyricum* and *Narcissus marinus africanus* which looks like a haemanthus and was another of the plants that did not survive. *Leucojum aestivum, autumnale, trichophyllum* and *vernum* are what we might expect, but *Polianthes tuberosa*, the tuberose, is rather a surprise at this early date and presumably did not survive.

A huge number of cvs of the hyacinth are illustrated, of different colours and both single and double. Other plants listed among the hyacinths are numerous muscari – *M.M. atlanticum, moschatum, plumosum* – and some bellevalias, *Dipcadi serotina* and a number of unidentifiable scillas as well as *S. liliohyacinthus, S. peruviana, Endymion hispanicus* and *Urginea maritima*. Ornithogalums are represented by *O. arabicum, O. pyrenaicum, O. narbonense, O. umbellatum* and one not easily identified. Quite a few *Allium* spp. were grown of which *A. triquetrum* and *Nothoscordum fragrans* are the most easily recognised. *Asphodelus ramosus, albus* and *fistulosus* and

Asphodeline lutea follow, after which come the two *Hemerocallis* species, *Paradisea liliastrum* and some anthericum, probably *A. ramosum.*

Not surprisingly, perhaps, crocus and colchicums got confused, and it is by no means easy to distinguish any of them. It looks, however, as though the list included *Colchicum autumnale, byzantinum, lusitanicum* (rather a surprise this), *parkinsonii,* and *variegatum, Merendera montana* and *Bulbocodium vernum.* Representing *Crocus* species proper there would appear to be *C. vernus* in various colours, the Dutch yellow, *C. susianus, C. biflorus* and *C. imperati,* while in the autumn they had *C. sativus, C. nudiflorus* and a white-flowered one, possibly *C. boryi.*

Bulbous irises included *Gynandriris sisyrinchium* and *Hermodactylus tuberosus,* as well as *II. planifolia, persica, xiphium, xiphioides* and *filifolia,* most of the xiphiums in various colours. Among rhizomatous irises we can identify *I. susiana, I. germanica* in various colours, *I. chamaeiris* (or *pumila,* or perhaps both), *I. pallida, I. variegata, I. graminifolia, I. spuria* and *I. aurea.* Although six kinds of gladiolus are mentioned, it would seem that they were all forms of either *G. byzantinus* or *G. segetum.* They had, according to Parkinson, the advantage of flowering late – in June and July – but 'if it be suffered any long time in a Garden, it will rather choak and pester it, than be an ornament unto it'.

The dog's tooth violet, *Erythronium dens-canis,* and the butterfly orchid, *Platanthera bifolia* come next, followed by a collection of cyclamens, of which *C. repandum, C. coum, C. creticum, C. europaeum* and *C. hederifolium* can be recognised. There is also a rather large-leafed one which might be either *C. graecum* or *C. persicum;* the text is not clear.

Now come the anemones, with a great variety of coronarias and hortensis cvs. Parkinson advises planting them at different seasons, some in the autumn others in the spring, to obtain a long season. He also grew *Pulsatilla vulgaris, P. alpina, Anemone ranunculoides, AA. trifolia, nemorosa fl.pl. silvestris* and *palmata.* The aconites in the list start off, rather disconcertingly, with the winter aconite, *Eranthis hiemalis* and are followed by *Aconitum napellus* and *A. lycoctonum.*

Now we come to the *Ranunculus* species, amongst which *Thalictrum tuberosum* has been wrongly placed. The others are various forms of *RR. asiaticus, aconitifolius* and *gramineus,* a white one, possibly *R. pyrenaica* and *Callianthemum coriandrifolium*. There were a number of cvs of *Hepatica triloba*, both colour variants and doubles being available. *Geraniums* seem to have been restricted to *GG. tuberosum, sanguineum* and *striatum*.

Among saxifragas were *S. aizoides* and four unidentifiable species. *Cortusa matthioli* had come into cultivation, and also a large number of primulas, which Parkinson divides into two sections, comprising bear's ears (auriculas), and primroses and cowslips. Most of the auriculas probably are just that, but *Auricula ursi flore et folio boraginis* (the bear's ear with flowers and leaves like a borage) turns out to be *Ramonda myconii*, while among the primroses and cowslips can be found *Primula farinosa*. Parkinson notes that it 'will hardly endure in our gardens for all the care and industry we can use to keep it', which proves that some things have not changed. There were three species of *Pulmonaria*, probably *PP. saccharata, officinalis* and *longifolia*; an *Echium*, probably *E. vulgare; Borago officinalis; Pentaglottis sempervirens*. A. *Limonium* or sea lavender was included, along with *Lychnis coronaria* and *L. chalcedonica*, a double, red *Silene* and one looking like *S. calabrica* or *S. armeria*. Both single and double wallflowers were there; various stocks; sweet rocket; honesty; *Oenothera biennis*, the evening primrose; *Anthirrhinum majus; Epilobium angustifolium; Linaria purpurea* and *Kochia scoparia,* the burning bush, which in those days was called Belvedere or Summer Cypress. The balsam, *Impatiens balsamina*, had arrived. There were a large number of colour variants of the columbine, *Aquilegia vulgaris*, as well as numerous double forms, while also included in this group were *Thalictrum aquilegifolium* and *Corydalis cava*. Larkspurs are presumably forms of *Consolida ajacis* and these were both single and double.

Tropaeolum majus was already available, but was it the same one as we now have? 'The whole flower hath a fine small scent, very pleasing, which being placed in the middle of some Carnations . . . (for they are in flower at the same time) make a delicate

Tussiemussie, as they call it . . . both for sight and scent.' Does *Tropaeolum majus* have a fine, small scent nowadays? Violas seem to be restricted to various forms of *V. odorata*, both violet and white, single and double, together with *V. tricolor* and *V. lutea*. *Epimedium alpinum* is, perhaps, a rather surprising plant to find at this time. Double opium poppies were popular and there was also a double red field poppy, now lost. There were three species of *Nigella* grown the popular *N. damascena* and also *N. hispanica* and *N. arvense*.

We now come to a mass of compositae, in the midst of which, for some obscure reason we find *Adonis vernus* and *A. autumnalis*. Apart from the great sunflower, it is not particularly easy to identify all the composites, but among them are *Achillea ptarmica* with double flowers; the double feverfew, *Chrysanthemum parthenium*; *Chrysanthemum coronarium*; *Calendula officinalis*; a plant that looks like *Tanacetum pallidum* (*Chrysanthemum hispanicum*); an Aster, though whether this is the European *A. amellus* or one of the Michaelmas daisies from N. America is not clear though it probably was *A. amellus*. *Tagetes* species, both the French and African marigolds had arrived from Mexico, double daisies, *Centaurea moschata* (sweet sultan) and three handsome thistles, which I am loth to identify. There were an enormous number of carnations, the best of which had been raised by Ralph Tuggie, and also a number of pinks and a few *Dianthus* species, among which are *D. superbus*, *D. barbatus*, Sweet William and the Deptford pink, *D. armeria*. There is a rather mysterious plant which Parkinson calls *Globularia lutea montana*, which looks like a *Globularia* in the illustration but which is said to have yellow daisies that smell like broom flowers. White and red scabious are described as well as various coloured corn flowers. *Acanthus mollis* and various *Eryngium* species follow, with *Dictamnus albus*.

Then we arrive at the Leguminosae. There are three annual lupins, white, blue and yellow, the everlasting Pea, *Lathyrus latifolius*; *Lathyrus orobus*; the asparagus pea, *Tetragonolobus*; *Hedysarum coronarium* (although the illustration looks more like sainfoin) and various medicagos grown for their odd fruits and called snails, thorny snails and half moons. *Paeonia mascula* and *P. officinalis* were listed plus the single red peony of Constantinople, which could be either *P. arietina* or *P. peregrina. Paeonia officinalis* was available both in single and double forms and coloured either red or pink. *Veratrum nigrom* and *Cypripedium calceolus* make an unexpected appearance, followed by *Helleborus niger* and another hellebore which may be *H. viridis.* There were both the ordinary white and the so-called red lilies-of-the-valley and quite a selection of gentians – *GG. lutea, asclepiadea, cruciata, acaulis* and *pneumonanthe.* Bouncing Bet, the double form of *Saponaria officinalis,* was already available.

Next come the campanulas, and, as well as single and double Canterbury bells, are blue and white *C. persicifolia, C. pyramidalis* and *C. latifolia,* while *Lobelia cardinalis* is included among the bellflowers. The plants known as *Convolvulus major* and *minor* were already in cultivation; *C. major (Pharbitis purpurea)* comes from tropical America and so does *P. hederacea* (*Convolvulus nil*) which was also available. Presumably they were Spanish introductions. *Convolvus minor* comes from the Mediterranean.

Why were Daturas so popular? Parkinson grew *D. metel, D. fastuosa* (from India), *D. tatula* and *D. stramonium.* A great novelty at the time was the marvel of Peru. There were a number of mallows, not easily identified, as well as single and double hollyhocks. There was the cockscomb, *Celosia cristata* and its var. *coccinea,* which had arrived from Asia as early as 1570, also *Amaranthus caudatus,* love-lies-bleeding, and *A. tricolor* (*A. gangeticus* var. *tricolor*) which is apparently recorded from 1548 by Turner. These both probably came from eastern Asia. The tobacco plant was grown for ornament at this time. There were a number of Mediterranean *Helichrysum* species, of which Parkinson lists four. He ends this section with a plant which he says was brought out of the West Indies 'and groweth plentifully in these gardens'. Since the plant is our native *Antennaria dioica,* this suggests that some enterprising nurseryman told a convincing tale. *Canna indica,* the Indian shot, was apparently grown quite extensively, although I am never sure how it was preserved from year to year. Perhaps the tubers were imported every year from the continent. This is followed by the mandrake and then by *Lycopersicum esculentum,* the love apple or tomato, which in those days was only grown for ornament. There were quite a number of foxgloves grown, including *Digitalis ferruginea, D. ambigua* and possibly *D. obscura*. The description of 'orange tawny foxglove' seems to fit this plant. Among the mulleins we can recognise *Verbascum blattaria* and *V. phoeniceum*. Was the great red deadnettle *Lamium orvala*? I think, almost certainly, that it was, as it is mentioned by Gerard. The valerian illustrated looks more like *Centranthus angustifolius* than *C. ruber* and probably both were available. So, also, was a true valerian, *V. tuberosa*. The double ladies' smock *Cardamine pratensis* was there as was candytuft, both the annual and a perennial species. The herbaceous plants end with the two periwinkles, *Vinca major* and *V. minor*.

Before going on to list the flowering shrubs, it might be as well to look back and see what might be expected to flower after June. There would be all the lilies; *Sternbergia lutea*; the autumnal narcissus (though they must have been very doubtful); *Pancratium maritimum*, again a doubtful flowerer; the tuberose would also be doubtful; *Urginea maritima*, the Sea Squill; *Hemerocallis* species; the colchicums and the autumn crocus; *Iris spuria* and *I. aurea*. The gladiolus is a possible inclusion, and also the autumnal cyclamen. *Geranium sanguineum* and *G. striatum* would probably persist a little beyond June, along with *Echium* and borage, the lychnis, the evening primrose, rosebay willow-herb, snapdragon, *Linaria, Kochia*, balsam and nasturtium. The double *Achillea* and feverfew. *Chrysanthemum coronarium*, the sunflower, *Aster amellus, Tagetes*, carnations, scabious, sweet sultan, *Eryngium, Dictamnus*, the thistles, the annual Lupins, the everlasting Pea and all the Gentians except acaulis would flower after June, and the double saponaria, *Campanula media* and *C. latifolia, Lobelia cardinalis, Pharbitis purpurea* and *P. hederacea*, the daturas, *Nicotiana*, the marvel of Peru, the mallows, the hollyhocks, the Celosias and *Amaranthus, Canna*, the autumnal mandrake, the tomato, the various *Digitalis* species, *Verbascum* and the *Centranthus*. It is not a bad list, although it leans heavily on annuals and half-hardy plants. None the less, it did mean that the garden could be considerably more floriferous. Two other plants that should be included here, although they appear among the list of shrubs,

5 New Place, Stratford. The garden of Parkinson's *Paradisus*: knots with spring bulbs

6 Stourhead. The eighteenth-century garden with no need for flowers

7 A modern recreation of the eighteenth-century wilderness

are *Asclepias syriaca* and *A. variegata,* both from N. America and probably slightly tender, but also fairly late-flowering. Gerard also mentions *Clematis recta* as a plant he grew and this should probably be included among the late-flowering plants along with *C. integrifolia* which Parkinson puts among the shrubs.

Indeed, *Clematis* lead off the shrub section with *C. viticella,* of which a double form was also known, *C. flammula* and *C. cirrhosa,* while *Passiflora coerulea* also comes here. This had been brought back by the Spaniards from S. America. Of daphnes, Parkinson had *Daphne mezereum, D. gnidium* and *D. cneorum.* Viburnums are divided between laurels, where *V. tinus* is found and other groups which included the Snowball tree, *V. opulus sterile.* Also among the laurels was the oleander and *Prunus laurocerasus,* the cherry laurel, a great standby of British gardens for many years. Another *Prunus* was the double form of the sour cherry, *Prunus acida.* The Honeysuckles are a difficult group to sort out from the illustrations, but they certainly include *Lonicera caprifolium, L. periclymenum* and *L. coerulea,* while *L. rubra* and *L. nigra* were also available. Whether *L. implexa* or *L. etrusca* were also present it is not easy to decide from either the text or illustrations.

Jasmines were restricted to *J. officinalis* and *J. fruticans.* There is also something that looks suspiciously like Solanum jasminoides, which could, in theory, have come from S. America, but which is not officially recorded until 1838. *Syringa vulgaris* in mauve and white is depicted and we know that *S. persica* was also present. *Philadephus coronarius* had arrived in 1596 but was not, apparently, very popular at this time. Then comes an infinity of roses, mostly gallicas and damascenas, but also single and double cinnamon roses; a double yellow rose, presumably the Double Persian, since it is noted as being very tender; the single yellow, which I imagine is *Rosa foetida,* the Austrian Yellow, a double rose without thorns, which sounds like a double form of *R. pendulina* and the late-flowering *R. moschata,* the musk rose.

Next come the *Cistus* species, which Parkinson calls the holly roses. He says that many were available but that he would only select the ones he considered best. It is as well, perhaps, to realise that Parkinson was not listing every plant that could be grown in gardens, but only those he considered most suitable. Among the *Cistus* species he mentions *C. incanus* and *C. ladaniferus* and a few others which are not easily identified, although we can be fairly sure they included *C. salviifolius* and *C. monspeliensis*. Now follow two plants described as *Ledum*. One is *Rhododendron ferrugineum* which all garden histories say was not introduced before 1752 although the illustration seems convincing enough to me. The other one is, I suppose, *Ledum palustre*, which also has an eighteenth-century date of introduction in such volumes as *Hortus Kewensis* and Sweet's *Hortus Britannicus*. Rosemary was not only recommended in itself, but there was also a variegated form, a broad-leaved form and a double-flowered form.

Parkinson observes that myrtles need 'extraordinary care and convenience withal to preserve them from the sharpness of our winters' and so he names only three, all of which turn out to be various forms of *M. communis*. The myrtle may be tender enough, but *Opuntia ficus-indica*, the prickly pear must have been even more so. On the other hand *Yucca gloriosa* will have proved reasonably hardy and given an exotic touch to any garden in which it was grown. The arbor vitae, *Thuya occidentalis* was, Parkinson tells us, brought over by the French. He compares it to the savin (*Juniperus sabina*) which was presumably also in gardens although not described by him. The laburnum was presumably *L. vulgare*. The Judas tree must have been present for a long time, as Parkinson mentions an enormous tree that stood in a garden at Battersea, which had belonged to Master Morgan, famous Apothecary to the late Queen Elizabeth. It is said to do best against a wall. There were a number of brooms, which are not easily identified, *Colutea arborescens* and *Spartium junceum*. The double pomegranate and the winter cherry, *Solanum pseudocapsicum*, are also listed.

Privet, although it was the native *Ligustrum vulgare*, not the Japanese *L. ovalifolium*, which we use nowadays, was employed 'for no other purpose but to make hedges or arbours in gardens etc, whereunto it is so apt, that no other can be like unto it to be cut, lead and drawn into what form one will, either of beasts, birds, or men armed or otherwise'. He shows two teucriums, as I have already mentioned, *T. fruticans* and probably *T. polium.* Two sorts of lavender, *Lavandula spica* and *L. stoechas* are included, along with *Santolina chamaecyparissus*, the most modern edging plant, hyssop, and several sorts of thyme, including one with variegated leaves. Parkinson does not normally describe trees, so although the *Robinia* and the horse chustnut were around at the time they get no mention.

Apart from roses, the early seventeenth-century garden was badly off for flowering shrubs and many in Parkinson's list are more or less tender. Lilac, laburnum, laurustinus, the snowball tree, cherry laurel, double cherry and various brooms do not add up to a very brilliant display. They had *Cornus mas*, of course, but this was grown in the fruit garden, not for ornament as it is today. The same must be said of *Berberis vulgaris*. Indeed the orchard was the place to see flowering shrubs with rowans, service tree, medlars, peaches, almonds as well as the more usual cherries, plums, pears and apples. Also the Bay tree was put in the orchard, although the Walnut was often put in the middle of great Courtyards.

To these shrubs should, apparently, be added *Tamarix anglica*, *T. gallica* and *T. (Myricaria) germanica*, plus *Hibiscus syriacus*. Parkinson does not mention the tamarisks, although both were known, and *T. anglica* had presumably even become naturalised by then. Possibly Parkinson did not think them sufficiently attractive. The hibiscus is an interesting plant. It exists in the wild in India and China, and presumably travelled to Persia by way of the Silk Road and thence to the Near East, whence it may have come with the real Turkish florists' flowers – hyacinths, tulips, Ranunculus, anemones and *Iris susiana* which had already altered the face of the flower garden. Some of these are said to have been brought back by the Crusaders, namely the scarlet *Ranunculas asiaticus* and the scarlet *Anemone coronaria*, although the story seems doubtful in the case of the latter as it appears to grow quite wild in Italy.

Rosa moschata, which may be native to Persia, seems to have come to Spain with the Moslems and spread from there. Sweet sultan and *Lilium chalcedonicum* will have come from Turkey, but a surprising number of the European flowers grown come from Spain and may well be due to Clusius's explorations there. The Mexican plants *Tagetes*, *Mirabilis*, *Polianthes* and *Yucca* certainly came from Spain, while the N. American plants seem to have come from France, although shortly the younger Tradescant was to bring plants back from this source. *Crocus susianus* was received by Clusius from Turkey, but it is native to the Caucasus, so must have been in cultivation already. *C. stellaris* seems to have been received at the same time, and may well be described among Parkinson's different forms of *C. susianus*.

Such, then, were the basic ingredients of the early seventeenth-century garden, but how were they displayed? The beds, as we have seen, were, according to Parkinson, mainly planted with the recent imports from Turkey, but also with other spring flowers, such as daffodils, crocuses and auriculas. Were the other plants he described planted in borders, possibly in front of the shrubs as in Bacon's garden? It seems likely. The herbaceous border and the shrub border never seem to have been put forward as novelties and, if you are going to grow flowers, this would seem the obvious place. The topiary work would, presumably, be confined to the geometric beds of the knot garden, and, since these were in evergreens, the garden would not lack attractiveness in winter. Whether, once the spring bulbs were over, they were replaced by summer-flowering plants we do not know. It seems an obvious thing to do, but I can find no mention of its being done. It may well be that the tender exotics, such as oleander and myrtle, were brought out of their winter, frost-proof quarters and the pots buried. The early illustrations certainly seem to suggest this, so that it may well be that these were placed in the knots, while the nasturtiums, balsams, marvels of Peru and carnations were planted in the trails.

I am sure that there must have been many gardens that were too small to go in for elaborate geometric designs and I suspect these to have been much like small gardens are nowadays – edged with borders and with one or two beds in the centre. Here, the flowers both shrubby and herbaceous would be in the encircling borders, while the beds might well have some topiary work, or, alternatively, they too could bear flowering plants. A breeder like Ralph Tuggie would convert his land into a nursery with his carnations lined out in rows as each year's seedlings came into flower, and he sought to see if there was a peer of his 'Princess' or his 'Rose Gilloflower'. Finally, I suspect that the garden of Nicholas Lete was full of choice rarities, planted in no sort of order, an arrangement somewhat like that of the Tradescants which is described in the next chapter.

3

The Seventeenth Century

THE LATER seventeenth century saw the introduction of quite a large number of fresh plants, mainly from N. America, but there were also the first introductions from S. Africa. These, presumably, came originally from Holland, although plants appeared in extraordinary ways. It was during the seventeenth century that, according to legend, a shipwreck caused the appearance of *Nerine sarniensis* on Jersey; a pleasant story which has recently been doubted. We know that the younger Tradescant brought back a number of plants from N. America and that later the Reverend John Banister was sending plants to Bishop Compton at Fulham. During the Commonwealth, there seems to have been considerable interest in flower growing by Royalists who had escaped persecution, but who felt that they would be safest in their country estates. So floriculture, particularly of the so-called florists' flowers, was taken up by a number of people.

The fashion in garden design, particularly after the Restoration, was taken from French models, most notably Le Notre, with everything in long, straight lines. Avenues would radiate in all directions from a central point and the parterre would be composed of square or rectangular beds – the scroll work of the earlier age would have appeared incongruous. Really grand gardens would probably be designed and planted by the firm of London and Wise, who appear to have been particularly successful in propagating hornbeams, so that hornbeam hedges were suddenly very widespread indeed. However, we should always bear in mind that the very grand garden was no more typical then than it is today and that the smaller garden was more likely to follow the fashion of the last generation.

We have rather more published sources for this period; most notably two catalogues of the Tradescants' garden in 1634 and in 1656. In addition we have *The Garden Book* of Sir John Hanmer, written in 1659 and the catalogue of William Lucas, which dates from about 1677. Although Sir John Hanmer does not give us any ideas about where the flowers were planted in the garden, he does give us instructions for growing and propagation, and it would appear that layering was a comparative novelty at that date. He also tells us how to preserve tender plants. 'Many plants,' he observes, 'which come to us from hot climates . . . must be kept in tubs or earthen vessels filled with earth to be transportable into places of safety as soon as the frosts begin to be dangerous.' He pointed out that a frost-proof room was not in itself sufficient. If the atmosphere were too close the plants would die and the same fate would occur if the plants did not receive plenty of light. What he was plainly advocating was the orangery.

However, the great amasser of plants after Parkinson was John Tradescant the elder who had been a professional gardener to the Cecils at Hatfield and subsequently to Charles I. He died in 1638 and was succeeded by his son who died in 1662. The younger Tradescant had made three voyages to Virginia – in 1637, 1642 and 1654 – and a number of plants were first introduced by him.

The older Tradescant possessed a copy of Parkinson's *Paradisus* and on the blank pages at the back he listed his new acquisitions each year. They are spelt in a very peculiar way and far from easy to identify. For example, the very first plant in the list is *Sittissos Amarantinum*. The first word is evidently *Cytisus*, so it is presumably a red broom. In the 1634 list this appears as *Cytisus maranthae*. Was this *Cytisus purpureus*? In 1629 he also received *Cotinus coggyria, Platanus orientalis*, a red honeysuckle, and a number of florists' flowers, chiefly anemones, ranunculi, tulips and roses (among which was the Austrian Copper) as well as one 'strange vine'.

In 1630 Tradescant acquired comparatively few new plants,

mainly tulips and narcissi, but also 'Semper eternum flore luteum', a yellow everlasting, and a night-scented geranium, thought to be *Pelargonium triste*. However, to make up for this comparative paucity, 1631 brought new plants in abundance. In the order in which he wrote them, there was *Lotus libica*, the lesser pile trefoil, according to the 1656 list; *Phyllyrea* (whether *P. angustifolia* or *P. latifolia* is not clear); *Sarsaparilla* (presumably a *Smilax*); *Smilax aspera, Pistacia lentiscus*; a shrubby *Artemisia*; *Cistus crispus* and *C. populifolius* and also a plant called *Cortusa americana*. I would imagine this to be *Dodecatheon meadia*, but the designation of *Tiarella cordifolia* has also been suggested for this plant. There are three Dentarias; one called *Herundelesie* I hesitate to identify. This is followed by *Sedum telephium*; *Molucca*, which is presumably *Molucella laevis*; a *Centaurium*; a white-flowered *Cyclamen*; three species of *Geranium*; *Euphorbia characias* (rather confusingly named *Tithemali caratius*); *Aristolochia pistolochia* and *Cneorum tricoccus*. This plant was known as widow's wail and seems to have been curiously popular in the seventeenth century. It was not particularly hardy and one would not think it particularly ornamental. *Amelanchier lobeli* turns out to be *Hedysarum coronarium*, which we have met already. There was a double-flowered *Philadelphus coronaria* and a mysterious *Caradathe Americana*. Whether this was the same as the *Carobe Americana* which appears in the later catalogues is not clear and this plant is more or less unidentified, although I would suspect it to be *Gleditsia* or *Gymnoclados*. Next come a couple of *Artemisias*, one with an umbellate flower and one with leaves like lavender; a tamarisk from Italy, *Lutea cretica*, which is said to be a woad from Crete, and so is probably an *Isatis* species and *Seseli aethiopicum*, which is probably *Bupleurum fruticosum* as it is described as a shrub in the 1656 catalogue. What *Feratium Indicum* was I do not know, and the lesser arum seems a bit dubious, though perhaps it was *Arisarum vulgare*. *Arundo Donax* also appeared in this year as well as a milfoil with yellow flowers and the American golden rod.

The year 1632 was not a particularly good year for the Tradescants. They obtained a white species of *Dictamnus*; a *Doronicum;* a *Eupatorium* from New Belgium, thought to be *Eupatorium ageratoides;* a perennial yellow poppy, probably

Meconopsis cambrica and a plant described as a Canadian shrub with a leaf like an *Epimedium*, which has been identified as *Ptelea trifoliata*. But 1633 was a bumper year of the plants acquired. *Androsace matthioli* may be the cortusa or some other alpine. *Ranunculus lusitanicus*, with a yellow, perfumed flower is rather obscure. *Colus jovis* is said to be the same plant as Jupiter's distaff, but what this is I cannot find out, unless it was *Lychnis flos-jovis*. What on earth was the great American poliferating tree daisy? Mea Allan in her book on the Tradescants suggests it is *Chrysanthemum serotinum*, whatever that may be. *Coepea lobeli*, Lobel's orpine is the annual Sedum *copaeum*. The next plant, aspeck, seems to be a *Lavenduia spica*, which could scarcely have been a novelty. A cyclamen from Antioch is intriguing. It does not seem to have been preserved to appear in later lists, so one might assume that it was the tender *C. persicum* or *C. libanoticum*. Two other cyclamen were received along with the one from Antioch, none of which are particularly identified in the later lists. What was the arborescent fumitory, with yellow flowers, evergreen and variegated? Was this just a variegated form of *Corydalis vulgaris*? *Asarum majus Americana* is thought to be *Asarum virginicum*, and in this year we first find mention of the white-flowered plant that was to be named in their honour, *Tradescantia virginica*.

What the true yellow Cretan polygon was I cannot suggest. *Polygonum* was a perfectly well-known plant name at the time, but a yellow-flowered one from Crete sounds unlikely. I suspect that arborescent meant something different to Tradescant than it does nowadays, as the yellow American arborescent violet could well be one of the yellow American violets, although it must be remembered that rocket was called *Viola matronalis*. In this bumper year other receipts were *Alchemilla vulgaris* and a plant which is called *Stellaria argentina*, which it is thought may have been *Phlox paniculata*. Since it is not listed in either of the later catalogues the matter is not very important. The tall *Filipendula* may well be *Filipendula rosea*.

The elder Tradescant obtained in this year a double-flowered *Ranunculus bulbosus*, four species of *Aster*, and a bulbous thistle from Montpellier. He also obtained some odd cyclamens. The one with a very fragrant, red, spring flower sounds like *C.*

repandum, but he also received two double cyclamens, one red and one white, which would be a novelty today, let alone in 1633. A yellow *Erythronium* must have been an American importation. It is suggested that *Gladiolus canadensis* refers to a *Sisyrinchium* species.

The arborescent sedum would, one imagines, be one of the aeoniums or greenovias from the Canaries. In the 1656 catalogue it is described as a tree houseleek. Clusius's *Cassia* is apparently *C. obovata*, the senna tree, which normally requires a warm greenhouse, although it seems to have survived until at least 1656. The arborescent *Hypericum*, the next of the 1633 acquisitions, could be almost any shrubby St John's Wort; according to the authorities it is most likely to have been the Cretan *H. hircinum*. *Mespilus arona* could well be *Aronia arbutifolia*, although this was not officially recorded as a receipt from N. America before 1700. *Anagyris foetida* has preserved its name, but after that we enter the realms of conjecture with *Piemetum realie*. Could this be the pimento? Was *Alipum motcsetie*[1] really *Globularia alypum*? *Jugibie arabum* sounds like the Jujube, *Zizypha jujuba*, but this is immediately followed by *Zizipha capadocia*. Possibly both entries refer to the same plant, which is said to have been introduced in 1640, and possibly it arrived with the next entry, which is the carob. Neither would have survived out-of-doors for long. *Mariaranum sempervirens* baffles me, but presumably *Sabina baccifera* is *Juniperus sabina* and *Phillyrea latifolius* is just that. Also received was the caper plant and, rather surprisingly in this list, *Soldanella alpina*. We end with three unknowns, *Sicorum grumosa radice*, *Gnaphalium marinum et Cotonuri vulgi sive Bumbax humilis* and *Philex baccifera*.[2] None of these names reappear in the later catalogues.

The great difference between the plants listed by Parkinson and those listed by the Tradescants lies mainly in the number of introductions from N. America. We know that the younger Tradescant visited Virginia in 1637, 1642 and 1654, and it is

[1] Mr. Harvey tells me that in Ree's Cyclopaedia for 1786 there is the following entry. 'Alypon Montis Ceti – White Turbith – a plant common in Provence and Languedoc, a sort of Senna.' Unfortunately neither Mr. Harvey nor I can identify White Turbith.

[2] *Philex* is possibly *Filix*, a fern, so the plant could be *Cystopreris bulbifera*, which might be thought of as bearing berries.

suggested that he might have made an earlier visit about 1631, so it may well be that the later additions are due to him. Of these, the most important, apart from those already listed are *Acer rubrum* and another *Acer*, thought by Mea Allan to be *Platanus occidentalis*, which Tradescant certainly had. But, since he was familiar with the Oriental plane, I cannot think that he would have confused it with a Maple and I would rather settle for *Acer negundo*, *Actaea alba*, the Virginian amaracock is some *Passiflora*, although whether *P. lutea* or *P. incarnata* seems doubtful. *Aquilegia virginiana* is probably *A. canadensis*. There were probably quite a few *Aster* species of which *A. tradescantii* is fairly certain, but there was also an earlier-flowering form and a later-flowering blue one. What was the Virginian woodbine tree? And what the Virginian convolvulus with a heart-shaped leaf and insignificant flowers (*flore obsoleto*)? *Ipomaea pandurata* is a Virginian plant, but the flowers are showy. The Cornus with red twigs and white berries was, I imagine, *C. stolonifera*, which must thus have arrived in cultivation considerably earlier than generally admitted. *Cornus amomum* was in cultivation in 1683, but this does not have red twigs nor white fruits, and so does not agree with Tradescant's description. Tradescant's Virginian cypress is almost certainly *Taxodium distichum*. The American *Doronicum* is thought to be a *Rudbeckia*, while the Virginian *Digitalis* with very narrow leaves is probably *Chelone glabra*.

The elucidation of Tradescant's names is rather tedious for the non-specialist, so it is easier just to list the American introductions in the 1656 catalogue, apart from those already mentioned. They include: *Mimosa pudica* (brought from Barbados according to Tradescant, whence also came the guava and a 'cabbage tree'); *Rhus toxicodendron* and *Rhus typhina*, poison ivy and the stag's horn sumach; the true Virginian creeper, *Parthenoissus quinquefolius*; *Celtis occidentalis*; *Monarda fistulosa*; a polygonum; possibly the tulip tree, *Liriodendron*; *Vitis labrusca* and *V. vulpina*; *Staphylea trifolia*; *Gelseminum sempervirens*; *Yucca filamentosa*; two Eupatorium species, one from New England and one from New Belgium; and *Lupinus perennis* which was an important novelty as until this time only annual lupins had been known. Other American imports were three plants that might have been either species of *Carya* or of *Juglans*, a *Geranium* species, a *Ranunculus* species, *Smilacina racemosa*, and possibly *Sarracenia purpurea, Asima triloba, Hamamelis virginiana* and *Xanthoxylum clava-herculis.* There was also a rather mysterious plant described as the large Virginian pyracantha, which was presumably a *Crataegus* and which was not evergreen unlike the other *Pyracantha* in cultivation, *P. coccinea.* Apart from some of the trees and shrubs this is not, perhaps, a list to fire the modern flower-lover's heart. Incidentally Sir John Hanmer says that the perennial lupin flowered in April and May – much earlier than today.

Tradescant's 1656 catalogue contains some 1,600 different plants, but includes a very large number that would not, nowadays, be regarded among garden plants, such as three species of nettle and five species of sorrel. Many of the plants listed are, not unnaturally, cultivars of the various florists' flowers of the period. There are, for example, twenty-three Anemones listed, five forms of *Hyacinthus orientalis*, thirty named tulips and seven ranunculi. There are also some definitely tender plants such as *Melia azedarach*, a prickly custard apple from Barbados, oleanders, and some others which probably included *Schinus molle*, a species which is certainly among Sir John Hanmer's plants. This survives around the Riviera, but could not have persisted for long in Britain, unless brought under cover each winter. It comes from S. America, so was presumably an early Spanish import; its introduction is said to date from 1597. Why it was introduced is not clear as it is not very ornamental. Possibly it was thought that the seeds would produce pepper, as it is still popularly known as the pepper tree. One of the main attractions of the American imports must have been their late flowering. Such plants as the monarda, the various asters and eupatoriums must have considerably enlarged the number of flowers available after June, which had hitherto been rather limited, while *Rhus typhina* and *Crataegus* must have added autumn colour in other ways.

Apart from the plants already listed, the 1656 catalogue includes *Arbutus unedo* and *Symphoricarpus orbiculatus.* (Or so I suppose. *S. orbiculatus* is listed as *Ascyrum vulgare*, ordinary St. Peter's wort and this was the common name for the snowberry in the eighteenth century. *Hortus Kewensis*, however, gives the name to *Hypericum tetrapterum*.) Other inclusions were *Punica granatum*; *Cypripedium calceolus*; *Adiantum capillus-veneris*; *Echinops sphaerocephalus*, a good late flowerer; a double cherry; three species of *Cerinthe*; *Actaea rubra*; *Bulbocodium vernum*; *Convolvulus althaeoides*, a red-flowered dandelion, possibly *Crepis rosea*. *Opuntia ficus-indica* seems to have survived well in those days, and the catalogue went on to *Osmunda regalis*; *Clematis recta*; *Fragaria virginiana*; a double *Philadelphus coronaria*; *Galega* in various colours. *Gentianella alpina helvetica* sounds as though it might be *G. verna*. What the Brazilian liquorice was I cannot think. Besides *Mimosa pudica*, he also had *M. sensitiva*. It looks as though *Colus jovis* is *Salvia glutinosa*.

Under the category *Hyacinthus* come a number of *Muscari* and *Scillas*, including *S. autumnalis* and some of these may have been fresh introductions. One would like to know what plant the winter hyacinth was. Tradescant had a large selection of henbanes and a number of unidentifiable hypericums. He had a number of double wallflowers, one with variegated leaves. Both *Laburnum vulgare* and *L. alpinum* were grown by him, but *Viburnum tinus*, *Danae racemosa* (only introduced in 1713 according to the authorities, who must have missed this entry under *Laurus*) and *Prunus lusitanica* are all new. Among the *Hemerocallis* species, then called *Liliasphodelus*, is one with a white flower; one would like to know what that was. The catalogue includes lichen and a number of mosses, including lycopodiums.

Lilium pyrenaicum seems to have swelled the ranks of these flowers and there was also a double *L. candidum*. He had *Celtis orientalis* as well as the American plant. Among the narcissi is one said to be from the Cape of Good Hope. Would this be the nerine? There is also one from Mount Carmel, which is even more unidentifiable. There were quite a number of *Ononis* species, of which one seems to have been *O. natrix*. Tradescant grew quite a few orchids, and one would like to know more of the one described as a yellow ladies' tresses. Apart from this he claimed he grew *Neottia nidus-avis* (presumably he dug one up and popped it in the garden and it was never seen again), *Ophrys apifera* and *O. insectifera*, various *Dactylorhiza* species and what he describes as hand orchis.

It comes as a surprise to find the various cowslips given the Latin name of *Paralysis*. There is a mysterious plant called *Ricinus austriaca flore phoeniceo*, the Palma-Christi of Austria or great spurge with vermilion flowers. *Ricinus communis* had been received in the sixteenth century, so I suppose that is what it was, although I cannot think how it was obtained so early. A very large number of the plants in this extensive list are, however, either herbs or plants that we should count as weeds, such as numerous thistles and chickweeds and plants that are pleasant enough when seen in the wild, such as basil, thyme and ladies' smock, but which are not usually grown in gardens. The Tradescants evidently wanted to grow one of everything and it was rather an embryo botanic garden than a flower garden that they were constructing. However they did manage to introduce a number of valuable plants.

Sir Thomas Hanmer's *Gardening Book* of 1659 was mainly concerned with flowers, although we still have no idea as to how and where they were planted. He did not suggest many plants that the Tradescants did not have, but there were a few, including numerous double forms of existing plants, such as a tazetta narcissus, *Lilium croceum*, a double Crown Imperial and a double greater celandine. There was a lily, which he describes as the Red Virginian lily. Was this *L. superbum* or *L. pardalinum*? In any case it seems to have been something new. Hanmer also grew no less than sixty cvs of *Iris xiphium*, the Spanish iris. Tradescant merely says that he grew 'several sorts' without particularising the various colour forms. I find this very interesting, for I certainly never realised that the Spanish iris had been cultivated for so long that various strains had been selected and propagated. They do not seem to have persisted for very long. Miller records only a few variants in 1758, but early in the nineteenth century they were available in countless named forms.

Hanmer certainly seems to have had *Narcissus triandrus* and possibly *N. cyclamineus* – it is not clear whether he refers to *N. cyclamineus* or to *N. triandrus concolor*. Hanmer had what he termed a gladiolus from the Cape of Good Hope with 'a very great netted bulbous root and light red, towards scarlet flowers, growing on both sides of the stalk'. This sounds like either *Antholyza aethiopica* or a *Watsonia* species, but there seem no

way of knowing now precisely what it was. Since it is comparatively easy to preserve the *Antholyza,* I feel that a *Watsonia* is
the more likely. Among orchids he grew *Orchis simia,* *O.
militaris, Himantoglossum hircinum* and some *Ophrys* species.
He also had a nearly black, single peony which is not easy to
identify. One thinks of *P. delavayi,* but that, of course, was
unknown for another 200 years.

A plant that has rather baffled all commentators on these early
plants is the white wallflower. It was quite widely grown, being
mentioned by Tradescant, Hanmer and Lucas. Hanmer, rather
exceptionally, says it was somewhat tender, which would seem
to exclude John Harvey's suggestion that it was *Arabis albida.*
Possibly it was the very pale sulphur wallflower, but this is no
more tender than any other wallflower. Miller calls the white
wallflower *Cheiranthus glaber,* which *Hortus Kewensis* puts
among the varieties of *Matthiola incana,* and would thus be a
form of stock. Miller says that the leaves have greater consistency
than those of any other sorts, and loose spikes of pure white
flowers that are especially fragrant in the evening or when the
sky is overcast. There was also a double form which was sometimes known as Prussian stock or Prussian ten weeks stock. Miller
says that the double sort needed protection from 'great rains and
frost in winter'. By the time Sweet came to publish his *Hortus
Britannicus* in 1830 it was called *Matthiola glabra,* the wallflower-
leaved stock, and he says it is illustrated both in Morison's
Historia and in Weinmann's *Phytanthoza.* By then it was also
available in red and purple as well as in white. It looks rather as
though it were the ancestor of the East Lothian stocks, as the
other strains, Brompton and Ten-week were already known.

A couple of other odd plants listed by Hanmer in his herbaceous collection are a pink *Hieracium* from Apulia, which is
possibly *Crepis rosea,* and a 'pretty Mountain Scabious with
white flowers and broad leaves like those of a primrose'. He also
had a plant wrich is either *Ipomaea quamoclit* or *Quamoclit
lobata,* probably the former, as we know that Parkinson had it.

It is when we come to the trees and shrubs that we see more
plants appear in Hanmer's list. These include *Eleagnus angustifolius; Cedrus libani; Quercus coccigera; Cupressus sempervirens;
Sassafras albidum; Phillyrea latifolia* and *P. angustifolia;* the

variegated *Rhamnus alaternus*; *Myrica gale* and the 'Coral Tree from America with fine red flowers, leaves in threes like a trefoil and very thorny branches'. This turns out to be *Erythrina corallodendron*, which is not supposed to have been introduced before 1691. Tradescant had only the narrow-leaved *Phillyrea* and no cedar of Lebanon, which must have arrived only a very short time before Hanmer drew up his list. The date usually given for its introduction is 1683, but this is far too late.

Of greater interest for our purpose is the *Catalogue of Plants and Seeds* offered by William Lucas in about 1677. This shows what plants were available to the ordinary gardener who might not list the Tradescants or the Hanmers among his friends but would have to go out and purchase whatever they needed. I shall not repeat all the plants we have already noted, but give some of his novelties. Among seeds could be obtained the matted pink (*Dianthus deltoides*), which was often used, according to Miller, as an edging to beds and the mountain pink which is in fact the Cheddar pink, *D. gratianopolitanus*. It is worth noting that *Aquilegia canadensis* was well established in commerce. Sweet scabious is easily identified, but what was Spanish scabious? Is London pride *Saxifraga umbrosa* at this early date? It would seem so, although we have had no previous mention of it, *Capsicum indicum* is rather vague. Venus' looking glass, *Specularia*, was available both in purple and in white, while Venus' navel wort (*Omphalodes linifolia*) was another plant available as seed. There was also an albino form of French honeysuckle, a plant that seems to have been lost. Fox tail may be a species of *Alopecurus*, though it seems rather strange that this should be offered as a flower seed. It is even more odd to find the Roman nettle, *Urtica pilulifera* being brought deliberately into cultivation, although it is not unattractive if you do not touch it.

Among the tree seeds were *Abies alba*, *Picea abies*, *Pinus pinaster*, *P. pinea* (?), *Juniperus bermudiana*, the Bermuda cedar, *Quercus ilex* and *Q. suber*, the cork oak, seeds of lime, laburnum and almonds.

Among the plants offered were all the florists' flowers, ranunculi, tulips, anemones, carnations, polyanthus and primrose, while among the auriculas were some double-flowered cvs. There was a double yellow Crown Imperial. Among the choice of paeonies were some coloured black, red, purple and striped. Red and white oleanders, *Medicago arborea*, *Cytisus sessilifolius*, hollies with white and yellow variegations and with yellow berries, the cedar of Lebanon, both the eastern and western planes, a variegated nightshade and a variegated woodbine were included, as well as most of the plants already listed.

The number of plants, including shrubs and trees that were available to gardeners by 1670 was thus somewhat larger than one might have imagined, and a good display could now be expected from spring until July, with a rather lesser choice for the latter part of the year. However, the first Michaelmas daisies must have given some interest to beds and borders late in the year, while the autumn was also being enlivened by the fruits of *Pyracantha* and at least one American *Crataegus*. More important, perhaps, for the larger gardens was the introduction of large evergreen trees, of which the cedar of Lebanon was to prove the most important, although the various pines, firs and spruces must have also added to the interest of the garden in winter. Among shrubs, the variegated hollies, *Rhamnus alaternus* and Laurustinus were significant, although they seem to have been eclipsed for some time by the two *Phillyreas*, which held a pre-eminence among evergreen shrubs for nearly two centuries. Today they are rare in gardens, but they are very attractive and should be seen more often. Among flowering trees, the increasing popularity of laburnum is easy to understand and, once it was seen in its glory, the horse chestnut must have seemed a great treasure. It is not easy to disentangle the various leguminous shrubs, but Spanish broom and bladder senna are clear enough and *Hibiscus syriacus* never lost its popularity. The English flower garden must have started to look not all that unlike what it does today. Flag irises, lupins and delphiniums were lacking, but quite a number of flowers were much as they are now.

—4—

The Eighteenth Century

As far as the flower garden is concerned, the latter part of the eighteenth century saw a very large influx of flowers, but this had, in reality, been going on throughout the century. The scene is dominated by four great plantsmen, Henry Compton, Peter Collinson, Dr. Fothergill and Sir Joseph Banks, with Philip Miller and William Sherard as two other notable figures. Moreover, towards the end of the century flower growing had become so popular that a very large number of nursery gardens were started and continued to thrive for many years. On the technical side, the gradual improvement in building and heating greenhouses meant that plants from the tropics could be grown with greater facility. At the same time, garden design turned from formality to informality.

At the opening of the century gardens were designed by London and Wise, strongly influenced by the work of Le Notre, with straight avenues radiating from a central spot – the so-called *Patte d'Oie*. Above this there would still be an elaborate geometrical parterre. This might have been planted with flowers but, when William III came to the throne, there began a great interest in the Dutch taste for topiary and the garden became full of evergreens carved fancifully into innumerable shapes, such as we can still see today at Levens and which roused the satire of Alexander Pope in his famous 'Essay on Verdant Sculpture' in the *Guardian*, in which the following exemplars are offered for sale.

'Adam and Eve in yew; Adam a little shattered by the fall of the tree of knowledge in the great storm. Eve and the serpent very flourishing ... St. George in box; his arm scarce long enough, but will be in condition to stick the dragon by next April ... Edward the Black Prince in cypress. A laurestine bear in blossom with a juniper hunter in berries . . . A queen Elizabeth in Phillyrea, a little inclining to the green sickness but of full growth. An old maid of honour in wormwood. Diverse eminent modern poets in bays, somewhat blighted ... A quickset hog, shot up into a porcupine, by its being forgot a week in rainy weather. A lavender pig with sage growing in his belly. Noah's Ark in holly, standing on the mount; the ribs a little damaged for want of water.' Apart from its satire this is interesting for the list of shrubs that were considered fit subjects for topiary work.

It was, indeed, the men of letters who first protested against the formal geometric garden that had for so long been held up as the *beau idéal* of design. Although, nowadays, both Pope's garden with its grotto at Twickenham and Shenstone's famous garden at the Leasowes appear somewhat formal to us with their statuary and stone seats, they were remarkably unusual at the time of their creation and, very probably, extremely attractive. I suppose the first blow may have been struck by Addison in his essay in the *Spectator* in 1711.

'I am one, you must know, who am looked upon as a humourist in gardening. I have several acres about my house, which I call my garden, and which a skilful gardener would not know what to call. It is a confusion of kitchen and parterre, orchard and flower garden, which lie so mixed and interwoven with one another, that if a foreigner, who had seen nothing of our country, should be conveyed into my garden at his first landing, he would look upon it as a natural wilderness, and one of the uncultivated parts of our country. My flowers grow up in several parts of the garden in the greatest luxuriancy and profusion. I am so far from being fond of any particular one, by reason of its rarity, that if I meet one in a field which pleases me, I give it a place in my garden. By this means, when a stranger walks with me, he is surprised to see several large spots of ground covered with ten thousand different colours, and has often singled out flowers he might have met with under a common hedge, in a field, or in a meadow, as some of the greatest beauties of the place. The only

method I observe in this particular is to range in the same
quarter the products of the same season, that they may make
their appearance together, and compose a picture of the greatest
variety. There is the same irregularity in my plantations, which
run into as great a wilderness as their natures will permit. I take
in none that do not naturally rejoice in the soil; and am pleased,
when I am walking in a labyrinth of my own raising, not to know
whether the next tree I shall meet with is an apple or oak; an elm
or a pear tree.'

But, although he may have admiringly drawn attention to his
own wit, Addison seems to have been quite happy with other
forms of gardens. 'I think there are as many kinds of gardening
as of poetry: your makers of parterres and flower-gardens are
epigrammatists and sonneteers in this art; contrivers of bowers
and grottoes, treillages and cascades are romance writers; Wise
and London are our heroic poets.'

It is interesting that the flower garden has already become a
separate department, although associated with the parterre.
Addison's method of planting together flowers that appear in
the same season, although it seems commonsense, was probably
quite a novel idea. As late as 1830 one finds a writer in Loudon's
Gardener's Magazine commending the French habit of associat-
ing together different flowering shrubs that bloomed at the same
time. He obviously considered it as a great improvement on
current practice.

The separation of the flower garden as a separate department
is emphasised in Hill's *Eden*, published in 1757. 'The Flower
Garden' he observes 'and the Pleasure Garden, though usually
considered as the same are properly distinct: we do not mean by
this that Flowers should not be planted in Pleasure Gardens; but
that there should beside this be a particular Piece of Ground for
the Beds of the select kinds.' In other words, besides the pleasure
garden there was what might almost be considered as a nursery
garden for the more select plants. Still, there were flowers in the
pleasure garden:

'Flowers will be a great Ornament to it, but they must not be
considered as the principal Object; nor must the rest of the
Disposition be subservient to them.

'The finest Kinds that bear the open Ground must be planted

here with the same regard to Light and Shade, Harmony of Colour and Variety that we have recommended in the Choice of Greens for the Grove: and as the Variety is vastly greater in this Case, Fancy has more free scope. True Lovers' Knots of Box are banished, with clipped Yews and Holly Pyramids; nor is the plain strait Border the proper Form for the Flower Ground. No Edge becomes a Flower-piece like that of the Grass Walk, and they never appear so well as when they follow Meanders, and rise in little Clumps and Clusters. This, modern Taste has found, and there is nothing in the Article of Gardening which does it so much Honour.'

This quotation not only shows us what the taste had become by 1757 – which, incidentally, is more in line with modern feeling than seems generally recognised – but it also throws some light on what must have existed before. We knew all about the embroidery work in box and the topiary, but it is interesting to learn that the flowers had been grown in the long 'strait' border. I am not sure whether we should read here 'strait' or 'straight'; possibly both meanings are intended and the border was both linear and narrow. Precisely when the long border came into fashion is not easy to determine, but it has always been an obvious place in which to grow herbaceous plants. Nineteenth-century writers refer frequently to the old-fashioned mixed border, usually with contumely as something which could no longer satisfy the modern taste. And one of the main innovations of Hibberd and later Robinson was the development of this old, mixed border into the herbaceous border of the latter half of the nineteenth and start of the twentieth century.

It is obvious enough, even in the brief extract I have quoted from *Eden*, that there had been a complete transformation from the formal geometric garden, which had existed, to a greater or lesser degree, since gardens were first cultivated for ornament rather than for use. Pope's *Epistle to the Earl of Burlington*, which was published in 1731 would seem to indicate the watershed of taste. 'Timon's Villa' is thus described:

> 'Lo, what huge heaps of littleness around!
> The whole a laboured Quarry above ground;
> Two cupids squirt before; a lake behind

Improves the keenness of the northern wind.
His gardens next your admiration call,
On every side you look, behold the wall!
No pleasing intricacies intervene,
No artful wildness to perplex the scene;
Grove nods at grove, each alley has a brother,
And half the platform just reflects the other.
The suffering eye inverted nature sees,
Trees cut to statues, statues thick as trees;'

In contrast to this, Burlington was advised:

'In all let nature never be forgot.
But treat the goddess like a modest fair,
Nor overdress, nor leave her wholly bare;
Let not each beauty ev'rywhere be spied,
Where half the skill is decently to hide.
He gains all points, who pleasingly confounds,
Surprises, varies, and conceals the bounds.
Consult the genius of the place in all;
That tells the waters or to rise, or fall;
Or helps the ambitious hill the heav'ns to scale,
Or scoops in circling theatres the vale;
Calls in the country, catches op'ning glades,
Joins willing woods, and varies shades from shades;
Now breaks, or now directs, th' intending lines;
Paints as you plant, and as you work, designs.'

'Paints as you plant' – the words are prophetic of the revolution in garden landscaping which we associate with such names as Bridgeman, Kent, Brown and Repton. These seem to have been initiated by the popularity of the paintings of Claude Lorraine and Poussin, to which later were to be added the wilder landscapes of such painters as Salvator Rosa. It was not just to coin a phrase that Loudon referred to this school of design as Picturesque. The best results of this school are still a delight, but those people who deplored the wholesale destruction of the earlier gardens were not so benighted as they seemed at the time. We get the impression that Hill's banishment of clipped yews and pyramids of holly was not because they were unattractive but because they were no longer modish. Garden design became a matter of fashion.

The great landscapers worked with land, water and trees and even these latter were used very selectively. As a general rule, Capability Brown used only elm, oak, beech, lime, plane, Scots pine and larch, with the cedar of Lebanon reserved for special effects. Flowers played no part in their designs and from our point of view their work is only to be seen in comparatively minor details, as in the adoption of the wavy line, a greater use of grass walks and also – a quite adventitious result – the adoption of the closely-planted shrubbery. This latter effect seems to have resulted from a misapprehension of Brown's intentions. He would often plant clumps of trees on the tops of hills, with the intention that when they were sufficiently established most would be removed, leaving a few isolated specimens. The others were only planted to nurse the specimen trees through their early stages. Unfortunately, Brown's instructions were not carried out, and his clump-topped hills became a sort of Brown signature which the master would have repudiated. In smaller gardens the clumped shrubbery seems to have been regarded as the best that the small man could do in the Brown tradition, although it may well be that here, too, the original shrubbery was probably more airy and less impacted than has resulted from a failure to thin plants out. It is not rare nowadays to find shrub plantings much too thick, owing to a refusal to remove plants when overcrowding sets in.

Hill seems to have had a smaller garden in mind than the sort of estate that the great landscapists would have been called for. But his principles are much the same, although he also shows some interest in what was thought to be the Chinese style of gardening, as described in the book by d'Attiret.

'If we look out into the Fields, we admire near about us the free growth of the Hedge and the fresh verdure of the Pasture. These let us imitate by giving the Trees their natural Wildness and by providing a Soil where every Thing will flourish; what charms us at a Distance in this wild View is the Inequality of the Ground and its various Cloathing.'

This is not all that is attractive, however:

'Besides these there are in Nature Objects of Disgust and

Horror, which yet may be introduced happily; burnt Hills and blasted Heaths and barren Rocks and the wild waste of Commons afford a contrast . . . These Objects therefore will be sure to please, but they must be introduced with a sparing Hand . . . they are the Discords in the Musick of Gardening.'

Such objects were, in Hill's opinion, the sort of thing that the Chinese would introduce, but, he says:

'Let us learn from them that the sudden Transition from agreeable to horrid; and from gay to gloomy is pleasing; but let us correct the untutored Wildness of their Imaginations by forming nothing beyond the laws of Nature.'

Indeed, when he comes down to more precise details in the laying out of the garden, Hill still sets up 'Nature' as the exemplar, and this would seem to be the habit of garden theorists throughout the ages.

'Let us again refer for the Rule of our Conduct to Nature, she is never so charming as where wildest. There is an easy Freedom and a pleasing Negligence in her Disposition, which charms because it is not regular . . . If any suppose by this that an artless Distribution of the Ground is what we direct . . . they err extremely. It is an Air of Irregularity we advise, not Irregularity itself; there requires more Art by far in this distribution than in any other; and there requires afterwards the great additional Labour of concealing it . . . Every Thing we see should be chosen for its place, though it seem the result of Accident; there should be Order in every place, though under the Aspect of wild Freedom, and a certain Harmony where there is the Aspect of Confusion.'

This might well pass for the credo of the garden designer of the present day, where a studied informality is usually called for. Hill was also extremely practical in his various recommendations. At a time when exotics were being killed by too much heat he wrote: 'Many plants are smothered in Stoves that would flourish in the Greenhouse; and many encumber the Greenhouse that would thrive in the open air.'

He was also very practical in his suggestions for planting a grove:

'A third part of the Trees usually allowed will be fully sufficient . . . their branches will spread the further, the more distant they are at the root.' And with regard to the selection of species: 'Good Painters in Landscape call Autumn the most agreeable Season . . . it is one of those Beauties in Nature we can easily improve by chusing for this Plantation such as have the finest Tincts and the greatest Diversity of them.' He also recommends that 'flowering shrubs should be planted to edge the walk'. From my small knowledge of garden writing of this period this is the only reference I know to selecting plants, among their other attributes, for autumn foliage.

Sir William Chambers put forward a number of gardening theories in his *Dissertation on Oriental Gardening*, which is not really about Chinese gardening at all, but an airing of somewhat unconventional theories, which evidently owe some debt to Hill.

'Open groves should be composed of evergreens, chiefly of pyramidal form, thinly planted . . . with flowering shrubs amongst them. Others consist of lofty spreading trees, whose foliage affords a shady retreat . . . The plants are never crowded together, sufficient room being left between them for sitting, or walking on the grass, which . . . in the spring is adorned with a great variety of early flowers, such as violets, crocusses, polyanthus and primroses; hyacinths, cowslips, snowdrops, daffodils and daisies. Some trees . . . are suffered to branch out from the very bottom of the stem upwards; others, for the sake of variety, have their stems bare; but far the greater number are surrounded with rose trees, sweet briars, honeysuckles, scarlet beans, nasturtiums, everlasting and sweet-scented peas; double blossomed briars, and other odoriferous shrubs, which beautify the barren part of the plants and perfume the air.'

Chambers had also given thought to the arrangement of flowers:

'Avoid all sudden transitions both with regard to dimension and colour; rising gently from the smallest flowers to hollyhocks, paeonies, sunflowers, carnation poppies and others of the boldest growth, and vary the tints by easy gradations from white, straw-colour, purple and incarnate, to the deepest blues and most brilliant crimsons and scarlets.' Moreover, he says, one can blend several roots together, whose leaves and flowers unite and compose one rich harmonious mass; such as the white and purple candytuft, larkspurs and mallows of various colours, double poppies, primroses, pinks and carnations and the same method can be used with flowering shrubs, blending white, red and variegated roses together; purple and white lilacs, yellow and white jasmines; altheas of various sorts and as many others as can with propriety unite.'

This all sounds very modern in its approach and it can be combined with an appreciation of textures. Here are Peter Collinson's thoughts on the subject:

'Everyone that would beautifully imitate nature, should well consider the diversity and growth of trees, the size and shape of leaves, and the many shades of green. To know how properly to mix them in planting is another manner of painting with living pencils, for greens properly disposed, throw in a mixture and contrast of lights and shades, which wonderfully enliven the pictures and which insensibly strike the senses with wonder and delight. The effects must be charming to see the dark green elm with the lighter shades of the lime and beech, or the yellowish green planes with the silver-leafed abele; the chestnut, the poplar, the acacia, the horse chestnut, *cum multis aliis*, when fanned by a gentle breeze, then how beautiful the contrast, how delightfully the lights and shades fall in to diversify the sylvan scene.'

The author of these percipient words, Peter Collinson (1694–1768) is one of the seminal figures in the development of the English flower garden. He was a Quaker and a master draper, but horticulture was his greatest interest and he had numerous correspondents in different parts of the globe who would send him seeds and plants. To mention the less important first he received plants from China from Père D'Incarville and Père Heberstein. Plants from Russia and Siberia came from Dr. Gmelin, Dr. Ammann, the English physician to the Czarina Dr. Mounsey and the owner of Siberian iron-mines Mr. Demidoff, while Dr. Alexander Russell sent plants from Aleppo. A large number of interesting plants were obtained from these correspondents, including *Ailanthus glandulosa, Koelreuteria paniculata, Broussonetia papyrifera, Delphinium grandiflorum, Gleditsia caspica, Fritillaria camschatica, Lilium pumilum, L. dauricum, Malus floribunda, Paeonia tenuifolia* and *Struthiopteris germanica*, to name the most popular, plus various *Caraganas* and *Rheum officinale*. Unlike other plantsmen, such as Henry

Compton and William Sherard, Collinson freely distributed his plants not only to fellow enthusiasts but also to the nurserymen Christopher Gray and James Gordon, so that his acquisitions became generally available.

Interesting though his correspondents were, there is one who overshadows the rest and he is best introduced in Collinson's own words, written in 1766.

'As the nobility and gentry have for some years past introduced a great variety of N. American trees, shrubs and flowers into their plantations, the present, as well as the next, generation, may be pleased to know at what time and by whom such abundance of the vegetable production of our colonies was naturalised in our climate . . . My . . . business brought me acquainted with persons that were native of Carolina, Virginia, Maryland, Pennsylvania and New England. My love for new and rare plants put me often in soliciting their acquaintance for seeds and plants from new countries. I used much import to very little purpose for . . . what was common with them but rare with us they did not think worth the sending. Thus I laboured in vain or to little purpose for some years and obtained but few seeds or plants . . .

'Thus affairs stood for some years longer; at last some more artful than the rest contrived to get rid of my importunities by recommending a person whose business it should be to gather seeds and send over plants. Accordingly John Bartram was recommended to me as a very proper person for that purpose, being a native of Pennsylvania with a numerous family, the profits arising from gathering seeds would enable him to support it. At first it was not thought that sending over would prove a trade, but, with the demand, the price was fixed at £5 5s. a box. Besides myself the next person that gave John Bartram encouragement was Lord Petre [Philip Miller at the Chelsea Physic Garden was also an original subscriber] . . . who continued to employ him from 1736–1740, when the orders of the Dukes of Richmond, Norfolk and Bedford began. Afterwards the taste for planting grew and the annual orders for boxes of seeds.'

Eventually, Bartram had sixty-one subscribers, and by the late 1760s an enormous number of plants from eastern N. America had been received and many were in general commerce. There had been collectors around before Bartram, but they did not collect much and generally did so for a very limited number of people. Thus Henry Compton, Bishop of London, had sent John Banister to Virginia as a missionary in 1685, where he remained until his early death in 1692. He sent his Bishop seeds of a number of attractive plants, such as *Abies balsamea, Aralia spinosa, Cornus amomum, Ceanothus americanus, Crataegus 'coccinea', Lindera benzoin, Gleditsia triacanthos, Liquidambar styraciflua, Magnolia virginiana, Mertensia virginica, Picea alba, Pinus nigra, P. taeda, Rhus copallina, Quercus coccinea, Rudbeckia purpurea, Physocarpus opulifolius* and *Onoclea sensibilis.*

Banister was followed by Mark Catesby, who was later to write and illustrate the attractive *Natural History of Carolina*. He was in Virginia from 1712 to 1719 and was financed – although paid only £20 a year – by a syndicate comprising William Sherard, Sir Hans Sloane, Dr. Richard Mead and the Duke of Chandos. He returned again to N. America in 1722 and stayed until 1726, with a visit to the Bahamas in the interim. Among his introductions the most important were various *Aster* species, *Catalpa bignonioides, Calycanthus floridus, Coreopsis lanceolata, Erythrina herbacea, Ilex cassine, Stewartia malachodendron, Wisteria frutescens* and, probably, *Canna glauca, Helianthus atrorubens, Liatris squarrosa* and *L. spicata, Lilium superbum, Phlox paniculata, Rosa carolina* and *R. foliolosa.* There were thus a number of interesting plants in cultivation before Bartram started his sendings, but they were confined to the gardens of a few enthusiastic plantsmen and were generally not available to the customers of the nurserymen. Bartram was to change that.

For their five guineas the subscribers got 105 packets of seed; so that they paid only 1s. a packet, which was not bad going. One of these lists survives in the British Museum and contains four *Pinus* species; *Tsuga canadensis*; tulip tree; a 'white ash'; *Magnolia virginiana*; four maples; two *Castanea* species; three birches; *Sassafras*; a beech; two *Cornus* species; a mulberry; *Juniperus virginiana*; a lime tree; twelve different oaks; *Nyssa sylvatica*; *Picea mariana*; *Cercis canadensis*; four *Carya* species; *Ceanothus americanus*; *Rhododendron maximum*; three so-called kalmias of which one was *Leiophyllum buxifolium*;

Myrica cerifera; an evergreen privet (*Osmanthus americanus?*); *Sambucus canadensis*; *Thuya occidentalis*; *Lindera benzoin*; *Clethra alnifolia*; *Asimina triloba*; *Celtis occidentalis*; *Epigaea*; *Chionanthus virginicus*; four *Rhus* species, including the very poisonous *R. venenata*; a hornbeam; three so-called andromedas; probably two leucothoes and *Lyonia mariana*; *Ilex verticillata*; a hydrangea; *Larix americana*; a silver-leafed alder and the common Pennsylvania alder; two *Prunus* species; a broad-leaved *Euonymus*; *Callicarpa americana*; *Ptelea trifoliata*; four *Crataegus* species; *Aralia spinosa*; *Cephalanthus occidentalis*; *Hamamelis virginiana*; *Liquidambar*; two walnuts; a white and a red *Spiraea*; *Gleditsia triacanthos*; *Platanus occidentalis*; *Celastrus scandens*; two *Rosa* species and six plants described as viburnum. We do not know what the germination results were, of course, for the list includes some plants that are not supposed to have been received until after Collinson's death.

Whatever the truth, the number of plants that Bartram sent, and that Collinson distributed, slowly but surely transformed the English flower garden. I suppose that the most important were the first American rhododendrons and the magnolias. Among these *Rhododendron viscosum* and *Magnolia virginiana* were already known, but to Bartram we probably owe *R. calendulaceum*, *R. nudiflorum* and *R. maximum*, as well as other ericaceous shrubs such as *Kalmia latifolia* and *K. angustifolia*, *Ledum buxifolium*, *Leucothoe racemosa*, *Stewartia pentagyna* and, probably, *Gordonia lasianthos*. Among the magnolias, *M. acuminata* and *M. tripetala* can almost certainly be ascribed to Bartram and the probability is in favour of *M. grandiflora*. Other well-known garden plants we owe to Bartram include the bergamot, *Monarda didyma*; *Liatris spicata*; *Actaea alba*; *A. rubra*; a large number of *Aster* species, *Calla palustris*, *Dodecatheon meadia* apparently lost to cultivation, but now reintroduced; *Iris cristata*; numerous *Phlox* species, including the dwarf *P. subulata*; *Baptisia australis*; *Coreopsis verticillata* and *C. aurea*; *Stokesia cyanea*; thirteen species of *Solidago* and four *Viola* species, including *V. pedata*, to name only those that are still in general cultivation. He also sent over a number of orchids, chiefly *Cypripediums* (*CC. candidum, acaule* and *parviflorum*) as the younger Collinson had a passion for terrestial orchids.

Among shrubs and trees still in cultivation may be mentioned *Aristolochia durior*, the Dutchman's Pipe; *Cornus canadensis*, *Chamaecyparis thyoides*; *Fraxinus caroliniana*; *Hydrangea arborescens*; *Vaccinium macrocarpon*; *Amelanchier canadensis* (or *laevis*); *Diervilla lutea; Gymnocladus; dioicus; Illicium floridanum*; *Lyonia ligustrina* and *Oxydendron arboreum* as well as the trees already enumerated and a number of American hollies.

For some years after 1764 a much less important collector from the point of view of new introductions was the Queen's Botanist, William Young, but he apparently got his plants over in good condition. In 1771, Dr. Fothergill wrote to Bartram's cousin, Humphry Marshall, who also sent plants over to England; 'William Young sends his plants over very safely by wrapping them up in moss and packing them pretty close in a box. They come thus very safe and we lose very few of them. He ties the moss in a ball about the roots, with a piece of packthread or matting, and hemp strings, and puts them so close as to prevent them from shaking about in the box. It is surprising how well they keep in this manner.'

Sending plants in the days before wardian cases was a perpetual problem as the specimens had to be sheltered from salt spray and from vermin. Only too often the plants arrived either rotten or devoured by rats. It was thus much easier to send seeds, although these cannot always have germinated very readily. We know, for example, that magnolia seeds very soon lose their viability if kept out of the soil for any length of time. There were other problems with seeds, which James Gordon, the nurseryman, solved. He had once been gardener to Lord Petre and so preserved the first camellias to be received in this country. They were originally sent to Lord Petre, who put them in his stove where, not surprisingly, they died. Before that, Gordon must have taken cuttings. Lord Petre's plants are said to have been single-flowered, but Gordon later offered double camellias, so either there had been bud-sports, which Gordon had rooted, or he had taken seed from the original plants and some of the seedlings had come double. We have a testimonial from Collinson's pen to Gordon. Writing in 1763 he said:

'But what shows his great knowledge and experience in vegetation is his way of raising the finest dusty seeds; before him I never knew of any man that could raise the dusty seeds of the Kalmias, Rhododendrons or Azaleas. These charming hardy shrubs, they except all others in his care, he furnished to every curious garden; all the nurserymen and gardeners come to him for them: and this year, after more than twenty years' trial he showed me the Loblolly Bay of Carolina coming up from seeds in a way not to be expected. This elegant evergreen is next in beauty to the Magnolias and his sagacity in raising all sorts of plants from cuttings, roots and layers surpasses all others by which our gardens are enriched with an infinite variety, and for many years I have been a little assistant to him in procuring seed and plants from all countries.'

The Loblolly Bay is the plant that Linnaeus was to name *Gordonia* in his honour. We shall be looking later at Gordon's catalogue.

An interesting sidelight on the interest that there must have been in garden plants in the 1760s lies in the fact that Collinson's last years were somewhat embittered by the number of plants that were stolen from his garden at Mill Hill. Incidentally, this is now Mill Hill School and some of Collinson's trees still survive there.

Another Quaker, and a great friend of Collinson's, was Dr. John Fothergill, a very distinguished medical practitioner of the day. He, too, dealt with John Bartram and his cousin Humphry Marshall and also financed a botanical voyage through the south-western United States for John's son William Bartram. He obtained little benefit from the trip, however, owing to the outbreak of the War of Independence. He was, perhaps more importantly, the first to bring the cultivation of alpines into general interest, as he and another enthusiastic medical botanist, Dr. Pitcairn, sent Thomas Blaikie to the Alps to collect plants and no less than thirty-two species are credited with having been introduced for the first time from this expedition. The list include some intractable plants such as *Ranunculus glacialis*, *Androsace alpina* and *A. helvetica* and a couple of *Pedicularis* species, as well as fairly difficult plants such as *Geum reptans*, *Camapanula cenisia* and *Gentiana bavarica*. One would dearly like to know how they fared. They are all listed in Aiton's

Hortus Kewensis as having been presented by Dr. Fothergill, but we know from the writings of a later curator of Kew, John Smith, that the mention of a plant in this book only meant that it had been received, not that it had survived. Be this as it may, the mounting of such an expedition does seem to suggest that some real attempt was being made to construct an alpine garden, which is quite surprising for a date as early as 1776. Incidentally, Blaikie collected in all no less than 440 items and the full list, which can be found in the *Diary of a Scotch Gardener at the French Court* reads like an alpine flora.

It seems to have been Fothergill who first thought of sending the breadfruit to the West Indies, although it was Sir Joseph Banks who actually put the matter into practice, thereby indirectly being responsible for the mutiny on the *Bounty*. Fothergill apparently did succeed in sending cinnamon and bamboo from China to the West Indies and he also sent plants of his tea tree, one of his greatest treasures, to the southern American states in the hope of starting a tea industry there.

Unfortunately, we have no idea of the way in which Fothergill's alpine garden was constructed, but we do know a bit about how he grew many of his American plants. Firstly, 'Under a north wall I have a good border made up of that kind of rich black turf-like soil, mixed with some sand, in which I find that most of the American plants thrive best. It has a few hours of the morning and evening sun, and is quite sheltered from the mid-day heats. It is well supplied with water during the summer; and the little shrubs and herbaceous plants have a good warm covering of dried fern thrown over them when the frosts set in. This is gradually removed when the spring advances, so that, as the plants are never frozen in the ground while they are young and tender, I do not lose any that come to me with any degree of life in them.'

Fothergill also seems to have had the first woodland garden, in the modern sense of the term. 'I have a little wilderness, which, when I bought the premises was full of old yew trees, laurels and weeds. I had it cleared, well dug and took up many trees, but left others standing for shelter. Among these I have planted Kalmias, Azaleas, all the Magnolias and most other hardy American shrubs. It is not quite eight years since I made a beginning, so that my plants must be considered but young ones; they are, however, extremely flourishing. I have an Umbrella tree [*Magnolia tripetala*] above twenty feet high, that flowers with me abundantly every spring; but the great Magnolia [*M. grandiflora*] has not yet flowered; it grows exceedingly fast; I shelter his top in the winter; he gains from half a yard to two feet in height every summer, and will ere long, I doubt not, repay my care with his beauty and fragrance.'

This association of ericaceous shrubs and magnolias was to persist through the nineteenth century and into the twentieth. Such a garden was called an American garden, even after many of the rhododendrons were of Chinese or Indian provenance, but by no means everyone adopted Fothergill's admirable idea of having shelter trees.

Collinson and Fothergill were primarily interested in attractive flowers, while the more scientific amassers of plants were rather liable to evince interest in plants regardless of their decorative value. Philip Miller of the Chelsea Physic Garden was zealous in obtaining new plants, but had a reputation of being extremely stingy about distributing them, so that if Miller lost a plant it was probably lost to cultivation until it was reintroduced. Nurserymen are said to have lurked on the banks of the Thames, below Chelsea, to rescue the seed-papers that Miller had flung into the river, in the hopes that a few seeds would still be adhering to them.

Less stingy, but by no means over-generous with their novelties were the gardeners at Kew, William Aiton and Sir Joseph Banks, but it is to Sir Joseph that we owe the first plant collecting expeditions to the more remote portions of the globe. Most of these were to districts where the bulk of the plants would require greenhouse cultivation in this country. The most spectacular was the two visits of Francis Masson to South Africa, in 1772 and 1786, which resulted in an enormous number of plants being received in cultivation for the first time, including no less than ninety species of *Erica*, as well as numerous ixias, nerines, gladioli and pelargoniums. However, most of these plants were only of interest to gardeners with greenhouses; the number of which increased considerably as the century advanced. There were very few countries or continents to which

Banks did not send collectors. Besides being extremely wealthy himself, he had the support of George III for the embellishment of Kew and the number of plants that were received by that establishment in the closing years of the eighteenth and early years of the nineteenth century is phenomenal.

Unfortunately, in about 1815 the expertise at Kew appeared to slacken. In that year, Banks and Aiton had sent Allan Cunningham and James Bowie to Brazil, whence some 500 packets of seed were sent, besides plants and bulbs, but very few of these seem to have been raised successfully. In the later years, too, Kew had a bad reputation for destroying surplus material rather than distributing it. Before that time much of the surplus material was obtained by the famous firm of Kennedy and Lee, who had themselves various correspondents in foreign parts, so that they were able to barter plants with Kew. A number of hardy plants were, however, secured from China through the agency of William Kerr who collected from Canton between 1804 and 1810. During this time he sent back, among others, *Lilum japonicum* and *L. tigrinum*; *Pieris japonica*; *Kerria japonica* and *Rosa banksiae*, while from him or from friends in the East India Company, Banks obtained tree paeonies, various cvs of *Paeonia albiflora*, *Magnolia conspicua* and *Hydrangea macrophylla*, all of which slowly circulated to the nurserymen and thence to the gardeners.

As the century closed and the nineteenth century dawned, plant collecting became more widespread as nurserymen found it was to their advantage to send out collectors. All of a sudden, the raising of plants became big business. It even affected the work of the landscape gardener. The work of Kent, Bridgeman and Brown had concentrated on large-scale landscape work, built mainly on grass, trees and water, but when Humphrey Repton came to landscape Ashridge he had to arrange for an arboretum of exotic trees, an American garden with magnolias, a grotto and garden for rock plants, a rosarium and a mount garden, in which a flat area was converted into a series of small hillocks. Exactly what the point of this last feature was, is not entirely clear, but it sounds like Bacon's wilderness, which was also, it will be recalled, covered with hillocks.

It is a sign of the evanescence of the flower garden that,

although the eighteenth century saw the first opening of the flood of new plants that was to occur throughout the next century, it would seem that a number of plants cultivated in the seventeenth century had been lost in the interim. Parkinson had had *Ramonda myconi*, but that had to be re-introduced in 1731, his *Rhododendron Ferrugineum* was lost and not seen again in English gardens until 1752, while *Ledum palustre* was re-introduced in 1762. As for *Narcissus cylamineus*, that had to wait until late in the nineteenth century before it was redis-covered and brought back into cultivation.

While new plants were being brought into cultivation, many people were busily engaged in improving the flowers already in cultivation, most notably the so-called florists' flowers. During the nineteenth century these were often the special property of the artisans and some were confined to certain trades and localities. The association between pinks and the weavers of Paisley is renowned, but it was not only artisans who indulged in florists' flowers and the various competitions they engendered. Good tulips would often cost several pounds a bulb, and for these there must have been if not more aristocratic, at least more monied purchasers.

In his third volume of *The Universal Botanist and Nursery-man*, Richard Weston quotes extensively from a catalogue of 1769 which lists the incredible number of about 1,100 named *Ranunculus*, 681 late tulips, 116 early tulips and 7 double tulips, 273 different double blue hyacinths, 125 double reds and 177 double pinks and double whites, 208 named anemones, and, most extraordinary of all, 132 different polyanthus narcissi, divided into 68 with white perianth and orange cup, 3 all white, and 61 yellow. In 1777 the white double hyacinths were divided according to the colour of the eyes; they could be white, with yellow, red, purple or flesh-coloured eyes; and by that time there were three double yellow hyacinths to add to the list. On the other hand, by that time the English and Spanish iris were no longer obtainable in so many named cvs, although they were to return in the next century.

The aim of the florist may be compared to someone growing incurved chrysanthemums today, as the chrysanthemum is still a florist's flower in the true meaning of the term. Here, the actual perfection of the flower is the object of the grower's care. The actual shape of the plant seems to have been of secondary interest, with the exception of plants such as the auricula and polyanthus in which the whole plant was exhibited. The qualities of the perfect flower were subject to a large number of arbitrary qualities, some of which seem rather senseless. For example, however good your auricula or polyanthus may have been, if the flower was pin-eyed, not thrum-eyed, it would not merit serious consideration. It is these unsatisfactory flowers that seem to have been of most benefit to the gardener in the long run as it was the imperfect flowers that were used to decorate the garden, as opposed to being cosseted in pots and frames.

The most salient example dates from the first half of the nineteenth century, when the pansy became a florists' flower. Here, the rules required a perfectly circular bloom with a ground colour and an edge and centre blotch in a contrasting colour. Any plant that did not conform to these rigid rules was termed a fancy pansy and thrown out. However, these irregularly blotched pansies attracted the interest of continental gardeners and an export trade in them grew up. Towards the middle of the century the show pansy had been developed as far as was possible and interest began to slacken among the florists, but the gardeners now started to show an interest in the fancy pansies and they had to be re-imported.

Similarly, no florist would have any interest in self-coloured tulips. These only became of interest when they were attacked by a virus and became striped. This was known as breaking and an extraordinary folklore sprang up as to how the self-coloured tulip, which was known as a 'breeder', could be induced to break. The best florists' tulips were very expensive; £5 5s. a bulb was by no means excessive, but the gardener who just wanted a bright spring display could purchase breeders and inferior tulips at a moderate fee – we have now reached the stage where the self-coloured tulip is in demand, while the old favourites are only available under the general headings of Rembrandts, Bizarres and Bybloemens. The show auricula still persists in a rather *recherché* circle, but the throw-outs, the so-called alpine auriculas still decorate the garden. The show anemone and the show ranunculus would seem to have vanished past recall and would have to be bred from scratch, but anemones and ranunculi still appear in the garden, although, judging from old illustrations, here the loss is considerable. The laced polyanthus is rare and not much thought of nowadays, but the polyanthus is continually being improved as a garden flower. Only the pink and the carnation seem to have changed little since the old days and neither fit very happily into the modern garden, although the actual flowers are as handsome as they ever were.

The eighteenth-century garden, then, was one with a much larger number of plants at the gardener's disposal, while the way the garden was arranged was in a manner considered to be more 'natural'. The beds were probably still carved out from the lawn to make an elaborate pattern if looked at from above, but, even so, the majority would be either rectangular or circular. The elaborate geometric patterns of the knot garden were gradually disappearing. Of course, when garden design became a question of fashion a large number of perfectly good gardens were destroyed because they were no longer in the modern taste. People did object to Brown's destruction of old avenues, but their protests were largely unheeded. Long, straight avenues were *démodé* and there was no arguing with that. If Hill's description is to be trusted, flowers were grouped in beds or in serpentine borders set in the lawn. The paths did not, apparently, have flowers on their edges, except when they went through plantations, where the trees would be edged with a border of flowering shrubs. If the garden were large enough, a section would be set aside for floriculture, but this would probably be extremely functional in outline, composed of rectangular beds with paths between, in which the flowers would be set with little regard for decoration as such, but simply to grow the flowers to the best of the gardener's ability. Although the flowers were not necessarily florists' flowers, the approach was similar; it was the individual flower, not the general effect that was the object of this exercise.

Obviously this was not the only way in which flowers were grown. Fothergill's border against the north wall, with its winter dressing of bracken, may have been primarily floricultural in conception, but could also have been ornamental, while his woodland garden would undoubtedly have been attractive.

It is known that a rock garden was constructed in the Chelsea Physic Garden, in which was incorporated various geological specimens brought by Joseph Banks from Iceland. But the plants included have never been made clear. If one looks up the various alpine plants that are listed in Miller's *Gardening Dictionary,* you find that his main, rather odd, recommendation is that they should be planted in the shade, but there is no suggestion that rocks are essential to their cultivation. It is a pity we do not know how Fothergill and Pitcairn treated their collection. I have always suspected that the Chelsea Rock Garden was chiefly intended for ferns, as Miller often recommends walls and the fissures of rocks in the cultivation of ferns, but since the rock garden was put up by Miller's successor Forsyth, we cannot be sure of that.

We can reinforce Hill's writings by seeing what Miller has to say about the wilderness. He was probably writing before Hill.

'Wildernesses should always be proportioned to the extent of the gardens in which they are made, that they may correspond in magnitude with the other parts of the garden, for it is very ridiculous to see a large Wilderness planted with tall trees in a small plot of ground; and, on the other hand, nothing can be more absurd than to see little paltry squares . . . of Wildnerness work in a magnificent large garden.'

They should not be situated 'so as to obstruct any distant prospect of the country, which should always be preserved wherever it can be obtained . . . but where the sight is confined within the limits of the garden for its situation, then there is nothing so agreeable to terminate the prospect, as a beautiful scene of the various kinds of trees judiciously planted; and if it is so contrived that the termination is planted circularly with the concave towards the sight, it will have a much better effect than if it end in straight lines or angles . . .

'The trees should also be adapted to the size of the plantation, for it is very absurd to see tall trees planted in small squares of a little garden; and so likewise, if in large designs the plantation has only small shrubs, it will have a mean appearance.

'The walks should not be entered immediately from those of the pleasure garden, but rather be led into a small private walk, which will render it more entertaining.

'The old formal method of contriving Wildernesses was to divide the whole compass of ground, either into squares, angles, circles or other figures, making the walks correspondent to them, planting the sides of the walks with hedges of Lime, Elm, Hornbeam &c. and the quarters within were planted with various kinds of tree promiscuously without order; but this can by no means be esteemed a judicious method, because first thereby there will be a great expense in keeping the hedges of a large Wilderness in good order by shearing them, which, instead of being beautiful, are rather the reverse; for as these parts of a garden should, in a great measure, be designed from nature, whatever has the stiff appearance of art, does by no means correspond therewith; besides these hedges are generally trained up so high, as to obstruct the sight from the stems of the tall trees . . . which ought never to be done.

'In the next place the walks are commonly made to intersect each other in angles, which also show too formal and trite for such plantations, and are by no means comparable to such walks as have the appearance of meanders or labyrinths, where the eye cannot discover more than twenty or thirty yards in length. These should now and then lead into an open piece of Grass; and if in the middle part of the Wilderness there is contrived a large opening, in the centre of which may be erected a dome or banquetting-house, surrounded with a green plat of Grass, it will be a considerable addition to the beauty of the place.

'From the sides of the walks and openings the trees should rise gradually above each other, to the middle of the quarter, where should always be planted the largest growing trees . . . it will have a very different effect from the common method, where the trees are planted large and small without order. In these plantations there may be planted next the walks and openings, Roses, Honeysuckles, Spiraea frutex and other kinds of low flowering shrubs, which may always be kept within compass; and at the foot of them, near the sides of the walks, may be planted Primroses, Violets, Daffodils and many other sorts of wood flowers, to appear as a natural wood. Behind these should be planted Syringas, Cytisuses, Althaea frutex, Mezereons and other flowering shrubs of a middle growth, which may be backed by other flowering shrubs of a large growth.

'In small gardens, where there is not room for these magnificent Wildernesses, there may be some rising clumps of evergreens, so designed as to make the ground appear much larger than it is in reality; and if in these there are some serpentine walks well contrived, it will greatly improve the places, and deceive those who are unacquainted with the ground as to its size.

'In Wildernesses there is but little trouble or expence after their first planting, which is an addition to their value; the only labour required is to keep the walks free of weeds. And in the quarters, if the weeds are hoed down three or four times in a summer, it will still add to their neatness. The trees should also be pruned to cut out all dead wood, or irregular branches, where they cross each other, and just to preserve them within due bounds; and, as was before observed, if the ground be slightly dug between the trees, it will greatly promote their vigour. This being the whole labour of a Wilderness, it is no wonder they are so generally esteemed, especially when we consider the pleasure they afford.'

I would suggest that this is a significant passage in garden literature. Miller's *Gardeners' Dictionary* was a very influential book in its day, passing through eight editions in Miller's lifetime, then being revised continually after his death. His wilderness is another early woodland garden, although we have seen that it was being adumbrated by Parkinson and Hanmer, while his 'rising clumps of evergreens' evidently presage the worst kind of Victorian shrubbery, although, as we shall see, it may well not have been so bad as we are inclined to think it. Miller's 'old formal method', with the trees concealed behind hedges is the 'bosquet' of the old gardens, which looks charming enough in old engravings, but which must have been rather tedious to perambulate more than once. If we had to try to single out the main difference between the gardens, before the natural revival and after, we might say that the older gardens were rather regarded as a single entity to be looked at from a central viewpoint, while the modern garden was intended to be walked round and viewed from many angles. This is, of course, an oversimplification, but not an excessive one. It has been pointed out that this shift of emphasis is the direct result of the English climate. Italy is hot and dry in the summer, so that walking, even in the shadiest alleys, was somewhat tedious, while central France could also be excessively hot in the summer. Excessive heat in England is a cause for comment and, more frequently, it is rather too chilly to loll on the terrace and observe the tapestried garden laid out before one's eyes.

It might seem, therefore, that the flower garden as we know it today, had to all intents and purposes been envisaged by the 1770s. We cannot prove this, but it seems to be implied by the various gardening writers of the time. However, the number of plants at the disposal of the gardeners of that time was still comparatively limited, although it showed a marked increase on the past century. Let us then, consider two of the leading nurserymen of the day: James Gordon, the recipient of seeds from Collinson and others and Christopher Gray, who had his own foreign correspondents.

The catalogue of Christopher Gray that I have been able to consult is dated 1755 and contains details of trees, shrubs and plants. Among the herbaceous plants and bulbs are wood anemones with blue, red and with double flowers; a white *Chelone* and a red one; a *Collinsonia*; five species of *Phlox*; four species of *Solidago*; *Spigelia marylandica* and a list of twelve *Crocus* species including a blue autumnal one in addition to the saffron *C. sativus*. I imagine that this was probably *C. nudiflorus*.

Among the new shrubs and trees are four American *Acers*, of which two are evidently *A. negundo* and *A. rubra*, while the other two are the mountain maple and the New England scarlet-flowering maple. Possibly this last was *A. saccharum*, the description scarlet referring not to the flowers but to the autumn leaves. Here, too, was the sorrel tree, *Oxydendrum arboreum*.

A plant described as *Anthospermum* is, presumably, a greenhouse plant, *A. aethiopicum*, an early import from S. Africa. *Aralia spinosa* had arrived from N. America late in the seventeenth century. The double arbutus sounds like a curiosity, which, I suspect was fairly soon lost. No less than four species of *Bignonia* from America were listed, of which one can only identify *Campsis radicans* with certainty. Gray gives generic names, but never specific ones, and in those days the term *Bignonia* covered a variety of genera in the family Bignoniaceae.

One of the others was probably *Tecoma stans*; a third was probably the somewhat tender *Doxantha capreolata*, the fourth I
have not identified. A plant called *Borbonia* is also described as
the black-berried bay and turns out to be the plant known in the
eighteenth and early nineteenth century as *Laurus borbonia*.
This was a S. American plant introduced in 1739 and presumably
only suitable for greenhouse work, as was also the next novelty
listed, *Bosea yervamora*, the golden rod tree from the Canaries.
I am rather dubious about the plant described as the Virginian
flowering hornbeam, although *Ostrya virginica* seems the most
suitable candidate. Two species of *Cassine* would seem to refer
to a couple of early S. African importations, *C. maurocenia* and
C. capensis. The next novelties are *Cercis canadensis* and
Chionanthus virginicus, after which are four uncertain American
species of *Cornus*. These would probably include *C. stolonifera*,
C. amomum and *C. florida*. *Diervilla lonicera* appears next,
followed by a *Diospyros*, which was probably *D. virginiana*
which had been around since 1629.

The Mediterranean flora now impinges with *Eleagnus
angustifolius* and *Ephedra*, which always seems a curious choice
for an ornamental. We return to N. America with an evergreen
Virginian euonymus, which is presumably *E. americanus*. Two
American *Fraxinus* species follow, of which *F. americana* and
F. acuminata seem the most likely from the introduction dates.
Rather oddly the 'Shrubby Horseshoe Geranium' now appears
among the shrubs. Was this *Pelargonium zonale*, which usually
does not have a very marked horseshoe, or is this an early zonal
hybrid? In the mid-nineteenth century writers refer to people
who have preserved old tall horseshoe geraniums, and the
impression is that they were very tall, scarlet, zonal hybrids.

The next shrubby novelties are all from N. America and
include *Asimina triloba*; *Hamamelis virginica*; *Itea virginica*;
five trees that could be either *Carya* or *Juglans* species,
Liquidambar styraciflua, a magnolia which could be either *M.
acuminata* or *M. tripetala* and a couple of interesting *Malus*
species. One is *M. coronaria* and the other was described as the
Carolina evergreen crab. This was probably *M. angustifolia*,
introduced as recently as 1750 and partially evergreen in mild
winters. No less than eight species of *Crataegus* from N. America

were listed, of which two had yellow fruits. One of these would have been *C. flavus*; the other could be *C. parviflorus* or *C. punctatus var aurea*. An *Amelanchier* of the *laevis-canadensis* group was also available. There were three different American bird cherries, of which two were almost certainly *Prunus virginiana* and *P. serotina*. The third one was an evergreen and known as bastard mahogany and its description seems to fit *P. caraliniana* which has always proved rather tender and does not seem to have been recorded before 1759. The scarlet *Pavia* is *Aesculus pavia*. This is followed by *Calycanthus floridus*, after which we have a list of twelve different oaks, of which no less than eight are N. American. Two plants that have dropped out of cultivation since 1755 are a double pear tree and another form which flowered twice a year. There were two species of *Smilax* from America, which may well have been *S. laurifolia* and *S. bona-nox*, there was a Lime from Carolina, which appears to have been *Tilia americana* or perhaps *T. heterophylla*. The last American species to be offered is *Vitis vulpina*, the fox grape.

The catalogue of James Gordon that I have been able to find was not dated, but from internal evidence probably originates from the late 1760s. It is a more extensive catalogue than Gray's, including not only plants, but also seeds and a large selection of bulbs. We start off with annual seeds among which are 'Painted Lady Sweet Peas', mignonette, Virginia stock and red and yellow zinnias. The red-flowered *Z. multiflora* is not supposed to have arrived before 1770, but this is probably incorrect.

The seeds of perennials include eight different American oaks, two American ashes, two birches, two bird cherries, *Castanea pumila* the chinquapin, four *Carya* species, four *Magnolia* species, *Hamamelis virginica*, the American black larch, the American lime, the scarlet and the sugar maples, the tupelo (*Nyssa sylvatica*) red and white azaleas, three species of *Kalmia* (but this may include *Rhododendron maximum*), *Gordonia lasianthos* and various others. Most of these reappear in the plant list, so need not detain us for the moment. Although the catalogue contained very many more plants than Gray's, the plants are mainly listed under their English names and are much harder to identify. Moreover shrubs, trees and herbaceous subjects are all mingled together in a confusing manner.

Taking the shrubs first and ignoring the plants already listed by Christopher Gray we have the hemlock spruce, *Tsuga canadenis* and a Chinese fir, which is probably *Thuya orientalis,* which had arrived in 1752, although it seems odd to call it a fir. Among the acers is *A. tartarica,* and he had a variegated horse chestnut. Not only did he list the double *Arbutus,* but also a scarlet one. This was presumably the var. *rubra.* Among the azaleas were an early blush, which is presumably *R. nudiflorum,* a dwarf red, a late blush and an early white that was sweet scented. It seems odd that *R. viscosum* is missing. There is a *Clethra,* presumably *C. alnifolia,* and the four American *Cornus* species are presumably the same as those offered by Gray.

Hydrangea quercifolia seems a novelty, and Gordon lists four magnolias, *MM. grandiflora, tripetala, virginiana* and *acuminata,* described rather oddly as blue-flowered. Even as late as Loudon's *Encyclopaedia of Gardening* (1824) *M. acuminata* was described as bluish, which makes one wonder if some special form was found by Bartram which had a tinge of blue in its flowers. The various American *Crataegus* species are difficult to identify except for *C. prunifolia.* The maple-leaved thorn and the Virginian azarole I find hard to identify, although I see that *C. cordata* (=*phaenopyrum*) was once known as *Mespilus acerifolia,* so that might well have been the maple-leaved thorn. Two kalmias follow, *K. latifolia* and *K. angustifolia;* then *Rhododendron maximum* and a rare blue *Rhododendron,* presumably *R. ponticum,* which had only arrived in 1763, though this is hard to imagine. What the Carolina ononis was I am not sure; it was available with white or with blue flowers and was presumably some low, shrubby, leguminous plant. Gordon had *Malus coronaria,* though not *M. angustifolia,* but he did have an orange-coloured Tartarian crab, which I imagine was *Malus prunifolia,* as seems to be the only Crab that might be described as Tartarian and which was available at the time (introduced 1758). There was a *Lonicera* described as Collinson's honeysuckle, which was probably some form of *L. sempervirens.* There were five American pines and seventeen different oaks were available, of which six came from America. There were six *Rhus* species, including *R. vernix,* and a *Stewartia,* presumably *S. malacho-dendron,* although the description as with oval serrate leaves rather suggests *S. pentagyna*, a species not supposed to have been introduced before 1785.

Among the herbaceous plants were fifteen *Aster* species, three cypripediums – the yellow English, the red flowering and the spotted. The spotted one sounds as though it ought to be *C. guttatum* which was not officially introduced before 1829. The red-flowering one could be *C. macranthus* or perhaps *C. spectabile*. I suppose it could be *C. acaule*, but, according to *Hortus Kewensis* this was not introduced before 1786. There was a *Hydrophyllum* species, although it is not clear whether this was *H. virginicum* or *H. canadense* and a *Heuchera*. The only species that is known to have been in cultivation in the eighteenth century is the rather unattractive *H. americana*, but it is quite possible that Bartram could have sent either *H. hispida* or *H. pubescens* to Collinson and it might be that he means one of these, although their official dates of introduction are in the 1820s. The relation of the pyrola, *Chimaphila maculata*, is an interesting plant to find in the catalogue. Bartram had sent it over in 1752. Gordon lists three American *Iris* species. The dwarf, light blue iris from Pittsburgh is probably *I. verna*. Is the parti-coloured American *Iris* with a crenated style *I. cristata* or *I. versicolor*? I suspect the latter as that will leave *I. cristata* to fill the role of dwarf early, sweet-scented Virginia iris. Gordon lists five species of Phlox. These would include *P. paniculata, P. divaricata* and others less easily identified today.

The American Water-Lily, *Nymphaea odorata* is unexpected at this date and is, indeed, not supposed to have arrived before 1786, which is an additional proof that the dates given by historians in volumes such as *Hortus Kewensis* and the compilations of Sweet and Loudon are by no means always correct and that a close study of contemporary catalogues might well cause some revision. An *Osteospermum* from Virginia causes problems. *Osteospermum* is a genus composed mainly of S. African composites with yellow daisies – possibly some species of *Coreopsis* is meant and *C. verticillata* would fill the bill. Is the sweet-scented paeony from Portugal, *P. broteroi*? If so, it must be making its first appearance in a catalogue. A rhubarb with palmate leaves suggests itself as *Rheum palmatum*, which is said to have been received in 1763, possibly through one of Collinson's

Chinese correspondents. Four species of *Rudbeckia* have quite a series of possibilities and might include the newly-introduced *R. digitata*. The four *Liatris* species were probably *LL. spicata, pycnostachya, scariosa* and *squarrosa*, a larger selection than is available nowadays. *Podophyllum peltatum*, although originally introduced as long ago as 1664, must have been re-introduced by Bartram and now makes its appearance. There were two *Sisyrinchium* species which sound like *S. anceps* and *S. bermudiana*, and no less than twenty-two species of *Solidago* to round off the list of herbaceous plants.

The catalogue now continues with florists' flowers and lists eighty-two named auriculas, forty-nine carnations, 308 double hyacinths and seventy-seven singles, ninety-six named anemones and – quite a novelty – thirty-four named fritillaries. All these had Dutch names, which suggests that they were, quite simply, imported. It is not possible to identify them, although it would seem that most were forms of *F. meleagris*. Crown Imperials were not included among these; they appear in a separate list of fifteen named sorts, including doubles and forms with varie-gated leaves. There were eighty-three early tulips, 392 late tulips and twenty double tulips. An unexpected note is found in ninety-one named cvs of English iris; most of these were priced between 6*d*. and 2*s*., but 'Pompeius magnus' cost 5*s*. per bulb. The list ends with 649 Ranunculi.

The existence of nurseries carrying such extensive a list must surely indicate the existence of a sufficient number of potential customers to make such expensive work profitable. And we have only considered two catalogues out of a potentially larger number. It would seem safe to assume that the theory that flowers were not much regarded as parts of the garden before the nineteenth century must be incorrect. I suspect that we may have been blinded by the extensive gardens, of which we have quite a lot of information. If you have a large acreage you will approach your garden in quite a different spirit from the culti-vation of a small area. So I think that we can assume, without excessive speculation, the existence of a number of households whose area of garden was quite unsuitable for the designs of Brown or of Repton and which, probably, did not differ wildly in design from any suburban garden of today. I suspect that then, as now, it was the smaller gardener who patronised and encouraged the nurserymen, especially in their cultivation of the rarer plants.

A further indication of the interest in plants in the latter half of the eighteenth century lies in the thefts from which Collinson suffered. Someone must have coveted his plants sufficiently to have broken the law. There may have indeed been more sinister motives at work. In his *Gardeners' Magazine* for 1830 Loudon reports that many nurserymen had reported thefts from their stocks and warned against purchasing cheap material, which, he inferred, might well have been stolen from reputable nurserymen. Possibly, much the same thing was happening in the 1760s, the more so, perhaps, as Collinson owned plants that were not in general circulation, so that stolen specimens could be offered to connoisseurs or even to nurserymen. This is all somewhat speculative, but what is certain is that as the eighteenth century closed, the growing of plants and trees for sale to the public had become a lucrative business. It had also become widespread and there were thriving nurseries in practically every large town in the kingdom. Individual prices were comparatively low. In the catalogue of John and George Telford of York for 1775 the most expensive shrub is *Rhododendron maximum* at 15s., a price it shared with *Magnolia virginiana*, but comparatively few subjects cost more than half a crown. Admittedly, labour was much cheaper in those days, but it could only have been possible to maintain lists so varied as most nurserymen offered in those days if sales were considerable.

A number of people created what were termed private botanic gardens. These consisted of a number of small square beds, and a description of one such, although dating as late as 1829, may give us some idea as to what the eighteenth-century flower garden was like on the larger estates. The garden in question was at Trelowarren in Cornwall and consisted of a square of nearly an acre, surrounded by a brick wall 16 ft. high. 'One half of the garden will be illustrative of the Linnaean arrangement; the other half of the natural arrangement of Jussieu as adopted by De Candolle. Each arrangement is surrounded by a border of 5 ft. in width, appropriated to the flowering of the more beautiful herbaceous plants, including annuals. Through the centre of the garden there is a gravel walk.' In the centre was a temple, which was certainly not an essential part of the arrangement. Each half of the garden was 'divided into thirty-six beds, each 2½ ft. wide, with an alley 1½ ft. wide edged with box and gravelled'. It was reckoned that each half could contain 1,000 species and where a number of species were available it would be possible to vary the plants grown, so that some 1,500 species might be grown altogether.

In each department 'care has been taken to limit the number of species of the more numerous genera to six, with the exception of Solidago, Aster, Helianthus, Cnicus, Carduus, and some others, where illustrations are necessary to decide the approximation of one species in relation to another of the same genus'. (*Gardeners' Magazine*, VI, p. 421.) I think it is probable that something in this line (not necessarily with scientific pretensions) may have characterised the flower gardens of the plantsmen of the day. This garden was 'directly annexed to a very beautiful and extensive pleasure-ground laid out in the old style of gardening'. It is not easy to decide, in 1829, whether the 'old style' was that of Kent and Brown or whether it dated back even earlier, but I would imagine that it was probably in the 'natural' fashion of Brown and Repton. Even in this scientific garden there was the wide herbaceous border surrounding the whole and this, I would suggest, is the sort of arrangement that the smaller gardener would have concentrated upon. It would probably have been somewhat wider and backed with flowering shrubs, while the central lawn would have been diversified with beds, possibly arranged symmetrically, or possibly designed to give a fictitious natural appearance as in Hill's meanders.

As the eighteenth century closed, new plants were becoming available every year, and so the chances of the flower garden becoming more varied increased, to reach its climax in the first half of the next century.

8 Mount Grove: an early nineteenth-century flower garden

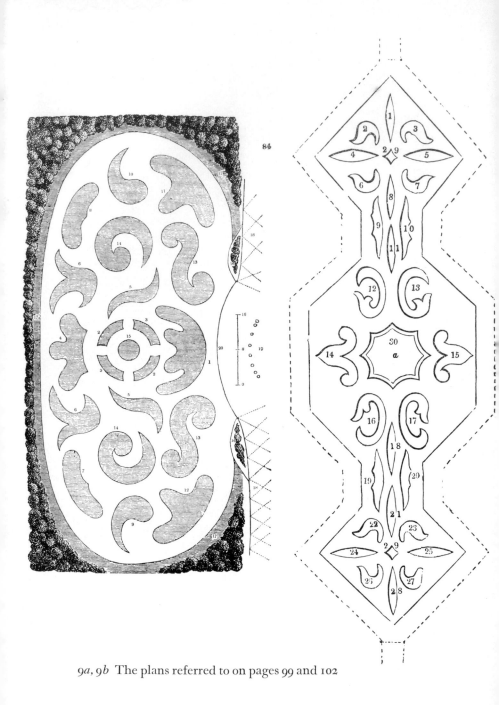

9a, 9b The plans referred to on pages 99 and 102

— 5 —

The Floral Explosion

In discussing the flower garden we have had to bear in mind, up to this point, the material that was available to the gardener but, once we reach the nineteenth century, the material becomes so extensive that all we can do is to list the more significant imports.

It was principally in this century that floriculture became important commercially, so that it was now worth nurserymen sending out their own collectors. The best-known of these is the house of Veitch, which, from 1840 to 1907 sent a very large number of collectors to various parts of the globe. The house of Veitch, though best-known of these enterprising nurserymen, was by no means the only one, although other expeditions are less well documented. For example, the firm of Loddiges presented an enormous list of plants in the early years of the century, including a very large number of original introductions, yet we know very few of the people who were originally responsible for these introductions, although it is known that a large number of missionaries collected for them.

The two most important collectors in the early years of the century were, in fact, nurserymen themselves. They were John Fraser and John Lyon who more or less completed the work of the Bartrams in exploring and sending back the flora of eastern N. America. Fraser's first collecting trips were in the 1780s and '90s, and he continued to collect until shortly before his death in 1811. Among his introductions are a number of well-known shrubs and trees, *Rhododendron catawbiense* and *RR. calendulaceum arborescens, canescens* and *punctatum*; *Aesculus parviflorus*; *Camassia esculenta*; *Carya cardiformis*, *C. glabra* and *C. paciniosa*; *Cypripedium pubescens*; *Eleagnus argenteus*; *Hydrangea quercifolia*; various *Liatris* species, *Magnolia fraseri*, *M. cordata* and *M. macrophylla*; *Nymphaea odorata*; five *Oenothera* species, numerous *Phlox* species; *Pyxidanthera barbulata* (one would like to know how long this intractable plant survived); twelve *Quercus* species; *Ribes aureum*; *Schizandra coccinea*; various *Vaccinium* species; *Uvularia grandiflora* and *Zenobia pulverulenta*, to name only those that have been introduced into general cultivation.

John Lyon tended to collect plants in large numbers. In his journal, one reads of 300 young plants of *Magnolia macrophylla* being collected in a single gathering and, since he was the last person to see *Franklinia alatamaha* in the wild (in 1803), one wonders if he was responsible for its eventual extinction. Many of his introductions parallel those of Fraser but it seems that he can be credited with *Chelone lyoni*, *Waldsteinia fragarioides*, *Dicentra eximia*, *Iris fulva*, *Jeffersonia diphylla*, and *Virgilia lutea*, again listing only those plants that have remained in cultivation. However, it is probably the actual numbers of plants of such species as *Halesia diptera* and various forms of *Rhododendron calendulaceum* that were more important to the gardening public. They had previously been introduced, but not in large quantities.

For the exploration of western North America, the gardener is mainly indebted to the Horticultural Society (it was not then the RHS) who sent David Douglas there from 1824–7, and again in 1829, while in 1846 another of their collectors, Theodore Hartweg, visited southern California. The third important collector in this region was Veitch's collector William Lobb, who arrived in 1849 and remained there until his death in 1863. There were, of course, other collectors, most notably John Jeffrey, but these three are the most important.

The number of plants introduced by Douglas is enormous, but here is a selection of the most notable : Three *Abies* species; *Acer circinatum* and *A. macrophylla*; *Arbutus menziesii*; four *Brodiaea* species; *Clarkia elegans* and *C. pulchella*; eight

Calochortus species; *Dendromecon rigidum*; *Eschscholzia californica* and *E. caespitosa*; various *Godetia* species; eighteen *Lupin* species of which *L. polyphyllus* was the most important; *Mimulus cardinalis*, *M. luteus* and *M. moschatus*; *Nemophila insignis*; six *Oenothera* species, sixteen *Pentstemon* species, *Picea sitchensis*; six *Pinus* species; eleven *Ribes* species, of which *R. sanguineum* and *R. speciosum* were the most significant and, of course, the Douglas fir, *Pseudotsuga menziesii*. It is hard to think of our gardens without the American currant and the lupin, clarkias and godetias, for all of which we have to thank Douglas.

Hartweg was able to introduce *Chrysolepis (Castanopsis) chrysophylla*, which Douglas had found but not imported; five *Ceanothus* species; *Cupressus goveniana* and *C. macrocarpa*; *Nemophila maculata*; *Nuttallia cerasiformis* and *Zauschneria californica*, and other, less popular plants. Of these the most important must have been *Cupressus macrocarpa* (grown at Chiswick in 1838) and the various *Ceanothus* species. Previously, Dr. Hinds, surgeon on the survey ship *Sulphur* had, in 1838, sent to Kew seed of *C. thyrsiflorus*, which was the first of the blue *Ceanothus* to be received in cultivation.

Besides further sendings of Douglas's best plants, William Lobb introduced *Abies bracteata*; *Aesculus californicus*; six further species of *Ceanothus*; *Chamaecyparis nootkatensis*; *Delphinium cardinale*; *Fremontia californica*; *Philadelphus californicus*; *Rhododendron californicum* and *R. occidentale*; *Thuya plicata* and the Wellingtonia, *Sequoiadendron giganteum*.

Mexico mainly yielded up its treasures through the sendings of individuals. Although Hartweg collected there for the Horticultural Society from 1836 to 38. *Salvia splendens* had been sent over in 1822 while *S. patens* arrived in 1838. This was not through Hartweg's instrumentality. He was responsible, if not for the first specimen, for the first large importation of *Fuchsia fulgens,* one of the main parents of the hybrid race.

From the Argentine the sendings were almost entirely the work of a freelance collector James Tweedie who sent seeds back from 1832 to 37. Among his sendings were the petunia and most of the parents of the hybrid bedding verbenas.

The other most fruitful source of garden plants from S.

America is Chile. Again, many of the first plants to arrive in Britain seem to have been sent by anonymous collectors. A Mr. Place seems to have had a number of contacts in Chile and it is thanks to him that the *Schizanthus* first beautified our greenhouses. James Anderson, the botanist attached to Captain King's survey sent back *Alstromeria aurantiaca* in 1830, at which time Hugh Cuming was collecting in the country. *A. haemantha* was received in the same year and *Libertia formosa* in 1831.

In 1843, and again two years later, Chile was visited by one of the greatest of the Veitch collectors, William Lobb, who brought back among other things, *Berberis darwinii*, *Escallonia macrantha*, *Embothrium coccineum*, *Philesia buxifolia*, *Lapageria rosea*, vast quantities of seed of the monkey puzzle tree and seeds of other conifers which have proved rather less satisfactory. Some fourteen years later, another Veitch collector Richard Pearce arrived in S. America. He is chiefly remembered for collecting all the parents of the race of tuberous begonias, but he also brought back *Eucryphia glutinosa* and *Berberidopsis corallina*.

The first regular sendings from India came from Dr. William Roxburgh in the early years of the nineteenth century, but these were entirely of greenhouse subjects. The first hardy plants came through the instrumentality of Nathaniel Wallich who was in charge of the Calcutta Botanic Garden from 1815 to 1847. During the whole of this time he was actively engaged in collecting plants and specimens and sending many to various correspondents. Even when he did not actually collect the plants himself he was probably instrumental in others doing so, and a large number of garden plants and trees can probably be attributed to his work, even though, on occasions, someone else obtained the credit for the introduction. Among his introductions were *Abies webbiana*; *Bergenia lingulata*; *Clematis montana*; *Cedrus deodara*; *Cotoneaster frigida*; *C. microphylla* and *C. rotundifolia*; *Geranium wallichianum*; *Iris decora*; *Morina longifolia*; *Luculia gratissima*; *Picea smithiana*; *Pinus wallichianus*; *Potentilla splendens*; *Rhododendron arboreum*, *R. campanulatum*, *R. barbatum* and *R. anthopogon*; *Rheum emodi*; *Rosa brunonii*; *Rubus pauciflorus* and *Tulipa stellata*. This list is almost certainly incomplete, and he was also responsible for the introduction of

Artemisia lactiflora, which he had received from his friend in Canton, John Reeves.

From 1823 to 1831 Dr. Hugh Royle was in charge of the hospital and botanic garden at Saharanpur in the Punjab. He encouraged the collection of plants in the Himalayas – in which practice he was also emulated by his successor Hugh Falconer – and sent back seeds and plants to the Royal Horticultural Society. The list of hardy plants thus obtained is quite large and includes *Androsace lanuginosa;* two *Berberis* species; *Bergenia ciliata;* the first *Codonopis; Deutzia corymbosa* and *D. staminea; Iris aurea* and *I. biglumis; Impatiens roylei; Leycesteria formosa; Potentilla argyrophylla* and *P. nepalensis; Primula denticulata; Pyracantha crenulata; Polygonum vacciniifolium; Sorbaria tomentosa* and *Syringa emodi.*

Between 1844 and 1850 Edward Madden, an officer in the Indian Army, was sending seeds and bulbs to the Glasnevin Garden in Dublin, among which were *Buddleia crispa, Cardiocrinum giganteum, Cassiope fastigiata, Lilium wallichianum* and a number of *Primula* and *Berberis* species.

The greatest volume of imports from the Himalayas came from Joseph Hooker's collections in 1849 and 50. Perhaps the most important fruit of this expedition was the collection of twenty-five *Rhododendron* species of which he brought back plants or seeds. These included such essential species as *RR. cinnabarinum, campylocarpum, ciliatum, falconeri, fulgens, glaucum, griffithianum, lanatum, lepidotum, triflorum, thomsonii* and *niveum* as well as some species of the Grande and Maddenii series. Apart from these, Hooker also introduced several *Berberis* species, three or four *Meconopsis* species, some primulas including *P. sikkimensis,* as well as various *Sorbus* species. He may also have introduced *Magnolia campbelliae* which he certainly saw and was highly impressed by.

A year later, Thomas Booth was sent out by his uncle, the botanist Thomas Nuttall, to search for rhododendrons in what the journals of the day referred to as Bhutan, but which seems to have been the Assam–Bhutanese border. From there came *Rhododendron keysii, RR. kendrickii, hookeri, smithii, shepherdii* and fresh material of various forms of species already known from Hooker's collectings or from earlier sendings

of Wallich. There were also a number of tender plants of which
R. nuttallii is the most spectacular.

With plants as variable as most rhododendrons the importation of abundant material is very valuable and it was thus worthwhile that sendings became duplicated. After this there seems to
have been comparatively little exploration of the Himalaya until
the present century, although amateurs were always sending
back the odd attractive plant.

We have already noted that Banks sent William Kerr to China,
but a better collection of Chinese plants came through the visits
of Robert Fortune. His first visit was in 1843 for the Horticultural Society, then came trips in 1848 for the East India Company, again in 1852 for the same company and in 1858 for an
American company who wished to have tea plants introduced to
the USA. After his trip for the Horticultural Society, who claimed
all his plants, Fortune sold them to various nurseries of which the
firm of Standish and Noble appears to have been the principal.
Among the enormous list of his introductions mention should
be made of *Akebia quinata*; *Anemone hupehensis*; *Clematis
lanuginosa* in several forms; *Cephalotaxus fortunei*; *Chamaerops
fortunei*; *Cryptomeria japonica*; *Daphne genkwa*; *Dielytra
spectabilis*; *Exochorda racemosa*; *Forsythia viridissima*; *Mahonia
japonica*; *Caryopteris mastacanthus*; double peaches and *Prunus
triloba*; *Platycodon grandiflorum*; *Pseudolarix amabilis*; *Rosa
sinica* and a number of rose cvs; *Spiraea pruniflora fl. pl.*;
Skimmia reecesiana and *S. japonica*; *Rhododendron fortunei*; *R.
obtusum* and *R. ovatum*; *Viburnum macrocephalum*; *V.
tomentosum plicatum*; *Weigela rosea*; *Wisteria sinensis alba*;
over thirty different tree paeonies; the pompone chrysanthemum
and various other garden plants.

After Fortune, until Wilson's expeditions at the start of the
century, the collecting of Chinese plants seems to have been
mainly the work of various French missionaries, but for most
of the century Fortune's sendings represented most of the
Chinese flora. However, numerous greenhouse plants, chiefly
azaleas, had been received through various East Indiamen
Captains, as well as roses, wisteria, *Paeonia lactiflora* cvs,
camellias, and magnolias, which arrived in the early years of the

century, often for the garden of Sir Abram Hume at Wormley-
bury in Hertfordshire. The plants slowly were propagated and
circulated but these importations were usually confined to single
gardens.

Japan was even later in giving of its botanical wealth, owing to
the fact that before 1860 no foreigners were allowed to travel in
Japan. Some Japanese plants did filter out, but very few until
Phillipp von Siebold arrived in 1823. Owing to his medical skill
he was allowed to travel away from the island of Deshima, where
hitherto all employees of the Dutch East India Company had
been confined and, until his banishment in 1829, he was able to
collect a number of plants and send them out. Even after his
banishment he seems to have received seeds from other employees
of the company. He returned in 1860 and sent further plants.
Among his introductions are *Deutzia gracilis*; *Euonymus
japonicus* and *E. radicans*; *Fatsia japonica*; *Hamamelis japonica*;
various *Hosta* species; *Iris kaempferi*; *Lilium speciosum*; *Lonicera
japonica variegata*; *Malus floribundus*; *Paulownia imperialis*;
Primula sieboldii; *Prunus serrulata* in various cvs; *Rhodotypos
kerrioides*; *Stachyurus praecox* and various cvs of *Thuya
orientalis*.

In 1860 both Robert Fortune and J. G. Veitch arrived in Japan,
and both sent back many plants including *Chamaecyparis
obtusa* and *C. pisifera* in several forms; a double *Clematis, C.
patens*; *Lilium auratum*; *Parthenocissus tricuspidatus*; *Sciado-
pitys verticillata*; *Thujopis dolabrata* from Veitch, while from
Fortune came various cvs of *Acer palmatum*; *Corylopsis parvi-
flora* and *C. spicata*; *Eleagnus pungens variegatus*; the male
plant of *Aucuba japonica*; cvs of *Clematis patens* and *C. florida*;
Primula japonica; cvs of *Prunus mume*; *Rhododendron metterni-
chii*; *Saxifraga fortunei*, a large number of *Chrysanthemum* cvs
and a number of variegated plants.

In 1877, Veitch sent Charles Maries to Japan to collect in the
more northerly islands, and among the many plants he brought
back were *Eleagnus macrophylla*; *Hamamelis mollis*; the lace-
cap hydrangea; *Stewartia pseudocamellia*; *Schizophragma
hydrangeoides*; *Styrax obassia* and *Viburnum tomentosum
mariesii*.

Subsequent collections from the area are of minor importance until the present century when a number of rhododendrons and cherries reached European and American gardens.

This broad outline gives the approximate dates at which the various denizens of the flower garden arrived in cultivation but is not, of course, the whole story. The early years of the nineteenth century not only witnessed a technological expansion in the Industrial Revolution but also a technological revolution in the application of cross breeding of species and varieties. Although as early as 1717 Thomas Fairchild had first (so far as is known) produced a deliberate hybrid with his mule pink, which was a crossing of the sweet William, *Dianthus barbatus*, with a carnation, this remained an isolated incident. Around the 1760s Koelreuter published observations on hybridising vegetables and towards the start of the nineteenth century T. A. Knight did a lot of valuable and spectacular work with fruits.

Precisely when the technique was applied to garden flowers is not easy to ascertain, although we know that Dean Herbert was working on *Narcissus* species in the 1820s in order to prove his thesis that certain so-called species were in point of fact natural hybrids. There are some *Pelargonium* hybrids dating from the end of the eighteenth century, but it would seem that hybridisation on a large scale took place in the 1820s. The genera most used at first appear to have been *Pelargonium* and *Hippeastrum* (*H.* × *johnsoni* dates from 1810). The *Pelargonium* crosses seem to have been mainly in the 'Regal' and 'Scented-leaved' sections and it is not quite clear when the original 'Zonal' hybrids were made, although they were in great demand in the 1840s and '50s. On the other hand, the pansy was being developed by Thompson in about 1813. He made crossings between three species, *Viola lutea*, *V. tricolor* and *V. altaica*. In the course of about twenty years the plant was transformed from a larger-flowered variant of *V. lutea* to the circular blooms of the modern plant. The biennial habit of *V. tricolor* seems to have been somewhat dominant and the plants had to be regularly propagated by cuttings. In Britain the pansy became a florists' flower and had to conform to rigid artificial rules, which severely limited the range of colours. Those that did not conform to these rules were, fortunately, exported, so that when the show pansy fell into desuetude, the 'fancy' pansies, hitherto condemned, could be reintroduced from the continent. They have retained their popularity ever since, without, however, any noticeable improvements taking place in the intervening century.

Once hybridisation had started it became a favourite pastime for amateurs and nurserymen alike, although true hybridisation, the crossing of one species with another, tended to be confused with the raising of cultivars from seminal variations from either hybrids or species.

It is hard for us nowadays to imagine the deluge of new plants that were depicted monthly in the gardening journals of the day. In 1838, the Reverend Henry Hill, writing in the *Floricultural Cabinet* could indulge in the kind of language that the early nineteenth century seems to have enjoyed: 'Ornamental plantations are now so universally spread over the face of this country, that our island may be compared to a vase emerging from the ocean, in which the Sylvans of every region have set their favourite plants, and the Flora of every climate poured her choicest gifts, for the embellishment of the spot round which Neptune throws his fostering arms.'

In the same number of the journal are described thirty flowers which were either newly introduced or newly bred. These were not only taken from the various botanical publications of the day such as the *Botanical Magazine*, the *Botanical Register*, etc., but were also supplied by such nurserymen as Loddiges, Rollisson, Young and Low, who specialised in the introduction of new plants. Growing plants was big business in those days: 'The common ash barberry (*Mahonia aquifolium*) . . . is a native of North America and was introduced in 1823. This species was ten guineas a plant as late as 1830, but plants may now (1839) be procured at 3s. 6d. or 5s. each.' (*Floricultural Cabinet* 1839, p. 245.)

The number of species that were either hybridised or 'improved' during the early years of the nineteenth century is extremely large. Most herbaceous growers today list three perennial lobelias, *LL. fulgens, cardinalis* and *syphilitica*, but in 1838 '*Clericus*' was describing a bed containing not only these three species, but twenty-one others, apart from an albino form of *L. syphilitica*. These were presumably hybrids, despite their Latin specific names, and ranged in colour from deep blood-red to various shades of purple, deep and 'glittering' blue, purple-crimson, scarlet, and sky blue. Of late, some growers have attempted to reproduce some of these early hybrids, but not with much success; the results have been principally a muddy purple, but possibly with perseverance these missing beauties may be revived.

A plant that seems to have been highly developed and then vanished back to its original species is the Pyrethrum. In *The Floral World* for 1869 Shirley Hibberd describes its development as depicted at Salter's Hammersmith Nursery. Mr. Salter, incidentally, was a rather remarkable figure who was quite prepared to let his enthusiasm take precedence over his business acumen and yet, in most cases, his persistence with an unpopular plant eventually paid off financially. It is to him that we owe the reintroduction of the 'fancy' pansy; he, it was, who, more than any other single man, encouraged the interest in variegated leaved plants; and it was he who persisted in growing 'Japanese' chrysanthemums, at a time when to most growers they appeared barbarously ragged.

'It is interesting to observe in Mr. Salter's charming plantations the various degrees of excellence in the varieties of pyrethrums. In the *Siberian Single* we have a pretty flower of a blush colour, the rays rather loose, the disk large, the attitude modest, yet pleasing. It is a very proper flower for the shrubbery, and might pass for a pretty homely weed . . . But herein is one of the foundation plants of a remarkable race and respect for genealogies compels us to notice it . . . When the florists had made a little improvement in the race and began to name them, the first that took a decisive place was one called the *Duchess of Brabant*, a fine bold single variety, the ray florets a lively rose-pink flower, the disk yellow. It was a long time before they became double, but as soon as a few good doubles were obtained, the single kinds sank into insignificance. Yet some of the earlier singles are worth having – as, for example, *Delhayii*, a nice rose-coloured flower; *Kleinholtz*, crimson and yellow; *Atro-sanguinea*, crimson; *Millerii*, rosy pink; *Tom Pouce,* red; *Striatum,* an inconstant and invariable (?) blush with rose stripes. All these have close hard gilt-button like disks and bold guard petals . . . but these are not all the singles that are worth notice, for in these

days of advancement there are at least two other later singles
that are worth notice and recommendation: namely *Prince
Albert*, a splendid variety with bold crimson rays and intense
golden-orange disk, superbly made and of great size; and
Delicata, which is "anemone-formed", with large guard, blooms
profusely, and is one of the most showy border flowers known.

'In the double varieties the guard is usually more compact, and
consists of shorter petals (ray-florets) which in the best overlap
slightly, so as to form an even and substantial annulus. The disk
consists of elegantly quilled florets, arranged in a solid hemis-
phere, and if the colours are good, flowers so formed are
extremely beautiful. The intermediate stage between the sheer
single and the thorough double is that form which bears the
name of "anemone", and which is the counterpart in this subject
of the class of flowers bearing the same name among chrysanthemums . . . One of the best of these is *Lysias*, which produces
a large number of bold flowers of the size of a crown-piece, the
colour a most pleasing shade of carmine. Others worth noticing
are the following: *Thomas Massart*, pale peach; *Comte de
Montbron*, pale rose; *Hendersonii*, rosy-purple, yellow centre;
Coqueterie, purplish-rose; *Vilmorin*, rose-pink with yellowish
centre.

'The next stage is the highest degree of perfection, and the
flowers of the third section are called "ranunculuses" on account
of their fine hemispherical outlines and the uniform character of
the florets, which are most elegantly and symmetrically arranged.
One of the best in this series is *Purple Prince*, the flower very
largely and finely formed; the colour rose, crimson and purple.
Haage & Schmidt, Titiens, Alfred Salter . . . are all grand in
character and may be called exhibition flowers.'

We know practically nothing nowadays of these elaborate
pyrethrums, although it is not easy to think of anything that has
taken their place. It would appear that culture may have had
something to do with the form of the flowers as according to *The
Floral World*: 'It is quite worth remarking, however, that in a
rich soil and abundance of water some of the anemone kinds
acquire ranunculus forms, and in starvation circumstances the
ranunculuses degenerate into anemones.' By 1869 the 'bedding
craze' was somewhat on the wane, but it was still fairly active.

For this purpose some dwarf pyrethrums were bred, among which Hibberd lists *Iveryana,* bright rose; *Nemesis,* dark rose; *Princess Alexandra,* white; *Carnea nana,* blush; *Tom Pouce,* red.

The above are just two examples of plants that were extensively developed in the nineteenth century and which now have dropped by the wayside, but this was also the century in which many of the popular garden flowers of today were also being created. Even the rose, which had always been among the most popular of garden flowers, was to be transformed by the introduction of remontant forms of *Rosa chinensis* and *R. gigantea* into cultivation at the end of the eighteenth and beginning of the nineteenth centuries. Oddly enough, *Rosa chinensis* seems to have been known in Europe for some time. It is shown in a painting by Bronzino, which has been assigned a date of 1529, while in 1578 Montaigne was shown a rose at Ferrara, which was said to flower continuously.

Although he does not mention it in his famous *Gardeners' Dictionary*, Philip Miller is said to have had a pink China rose in 1750 and he is also said to have had a deep red form. These appear to have been lost and it is with 'Parson's Pink China', sent to Joseph Banks in 1789 and flowered by Mr. Parsons in 1793 that the first remontant rose entered into general cultivation, closely followed by 'Slater's Crimson China', which brought a new colour into roses, but which, owing to its triploid character was not much use for breeding. The other two importations from China, from where it is thought that nearly all our modern roses originate, were 'Hume's Blush Tea-scented China', which was received in 1809 and which looks remarkably like a modern tea rose and the 'Yellow Tea-scented China', which was brought back for the London (later Royal) Horticultural Society by their collector Mr. Parks in 1824. Although both 'Parson's Pink' and 'Hume's Blush' are thought to have had the yellow-flowered *R. gigantea* in their ancestry, Parks's plant was the first true yellow among the remontants.

These early remontant roses were the parent of the Noisette rose, raised by a M. Noisette. In the meantime, on the island of Bourbon in the Seychelles, a second race of remontant roses appears to have arisen spontaneously through the crossing of the old 'Autumn Damask' rose (which may have been *R. gallica* ×

R. moschata) with 'Parson's Pink China'. These gave rise to the race known as Bourbon roses, which were less rampant, although still sizeable shrubs, usually needing support.

During the 1830s, the China roses were crossed with any other rose that would accept the pollen and the resulting plants were known as Hybrid Chinas. Since the remontant strain in the Chinas is recessive, the results were disappointing from the breeders' points of view, but these Hybrid Chinas, when crossed with Noisette, Bourbon or remontant China roses, gave rise to the roses known as Hybrid Perpetuals which flowered with considerable abundance but on very long shoots which had to be pegged down when planted out in beds. Crossed with the Tea Roses, the race of Hybrid Teas was evolved of which 'La France' (1862) is said to have been the first. At the close of the century the breeder Pernet-Ducher succeeded in introducing the yellow and bi-coloured *Rosa foetida* into the Hybrid Teas, while in 1924 the Danish breeder Poulsen crossed the 'Polyantha' rose (*R. multiflora* × *R. chinensis lawranceana*) with the H.T. to found the race known as Floribunda.

It was the breeding of the Hybrid Tea rose that gave the final *coup de grace* to the 'bedding craze', although there had been a reaction against it as early as 1858, if not sooner. However, more of that later; at the moment we are concerned with the plethora of flowers both natural and 'improved' that greeted the nineteenth-century gardener.

Sometimes the hybridisation seems to have been the result of rather unexpected causes. In the *Philosophical Journal* for July 1830, the Professor of Botany at Edinburgh wrote: 'Mr. Morrison, gardener . . . being aware that several of the finest species of Calceolaria were shy in producing seed, suspected that this defect might be corrected by applying the pollen of certain kinds to the stigmata of others; and he first has had the merit of presenting to the florist hybrids thus produced, which equal, if they do not surpass, in beauty, any of the species of this handsome genus. Mr. Morrison's experiments have been confined to four species, all herbaceous, viz. *C. corymbosa*, *C. arachnoidea*, *C. plantaginea* and *C. fothergillii*. He has succeeded in crossing the whole of these. *C. plantaginea* he finds most apt to produce seeds of itself and most readily to fertilise others.' Mr. Morrison sent

four hybrids to the Edinburgh Botanic Garden, of which the
plant of *C. fothergillii* (a dwarf species from the Falkland
Islands) pollinated by *C. corymbosa*, must have been remarkable.

Although this was stated to be the first time that calceolarias
were hybridised, it would seem that simultaneously, Mr. Penny,
the foreman of Young's famous nursery at Epsom, was also
engaged in this pursuit and was soon followed by other nurserymen, so that by the mid-1830s there were a large number of
hybrid calceolaries available, in a variety of colours and of both
shrubby and herbaceous habit.

Endless lists tend to be rather tedious, but it is necessary to
realise the enormous supply of flowers that suddenly became
available in the first half of the nineteenth century. In the *Floricultural Cabine*t for 1841 there is an article (like most of those in
the journal it is written under a pseudonym) in which twenty-
seven new seedling cinerarias are described and stated to be vastly
superior to the thirteen 'older varieties' which are also listed. The
colours ranged from light blue through lilac, peach blossom,
light and dark crimson, dark puce, white and purple, light
mottled, light and rose with blue edge to the petals. These were
all raised by Mr. Joseph Smith at Westerham in Kent, who was
apparently the foremost breeder of the day. The plants were
propagated by cuttings taken from offsets.

The so-called 'German' irises arose originally from natural
hybrids between *Iris pallida* and *I. variegata*, and their systematic
breeding would seem to date from 1800 when a Herr von Berg
of Neuenkirchen took up their breeding in an amateur way,
while M. de Bure of Paris took them up commercially. One of
his plants, a rather stippled light and dark violet called 'Buriensis'
may still be seen occasionally. Breeding continued in France
under M. Lemon, who was offering a hundred named cvs by 1840
and who continued producing new irises for fifteen years, so that
it is principally to him that the 'German' iris owes its popularity
as a garden plant. The race was improved, although this is argu-
able, by the importations by Sir Michael Foster, a great amateur
grower of irises, at the end of the century of a number of tall
bearded irises, which turned out to be tetraploids. When these
were bred into the existing hybrids plants of much greater size
were produced. Attempts have since been made to breed the

spectacular Oncocyclus irises to the 'Tall Bearded' varieties but
with only limited success.

We have already seen that there were a very large number of
cvs of the English iris, *I. xiphioides*. In the *Floricultural Cabinet*
for November 1842 are listed seventy-six cvs of *I. xiphioides* and
fifty of *I. xiphium*, all with brief descriptions, which suggest that
a great deal has been lost in the interim. For example, 'Adonis'
was blue, yellow and violet, 'Emperor' was purple and rose,
'Major' was purple-red, 'Princess Royal' was rose-spotted and
'Washington' was rose and white. The bulbs cost from 6*d*. to 9*d*.
each. There is also a list of fifty Spanish irises among which
'Cato' was white and green and 'Christine' was purple, green and
yellow. 'Hebe' was green, yellow and purple and a large number
were described as being feuillemort in colour, which I imagine
corresponds to the modern bronze shades, although 'Reine
d'Ispahan' is described as brown, while 'Nimrod' was orange.
This, presumably, was intentional, as a large number of cvs are
described as yellow.

From about 1813 the florists' flower *par excellence* was the
dahlia and the number of named cvs became ridiculous. The
original, significant importation was made by Humboldt in 1804,
presumably from plants that had already long been cultivated
in Mexico, and by 1830 there were at least 1,500 named varieties,
single, semi-double, double, 'Fancy' Dahlias with striped petals,
dwarf dahlias, while in 1830 Anemone-centred Dahlias appeared
and the small-flowered pompom dahlias had also been bred.
There was little advance thereafter until 1874 when the firm of
Anton Roozen was able to distribute the narrow-petalled plant
known as *D. juarezii*, which, when bred into the existing strain,
gave rise to the 'Cactus' dahlia. Colours in the 1830s ranged from
white (which always seems to have been rather rare) to blush,
salmon, yellow, orange (also an unusual colour), lilac and purple,
orange-scarlet, crimson and maroon, while 'Eclipse' was a
'beautiful fawn colour', and 'Richmond' was a 'beautiful bronzy
pink'. The majority of cvs were laced, that is to say that the
petals were tipped with another colour; for example, 'Lucina'
was 'white, laced with violet'.

The *Fuchsia* had been known since 1793, when James Lee had
distributed the Brazilian *F. coccinea*, a plant that is nearly

hardy, but probably no longer in cultivation. In 1823 the hardy and popular *F. magellanica* arrived from Chile, and this not only proved somewhat variable, but also was hybridised, whether intentionally or otherwise is not clear, with *F. coccinea*. By 1834, one nurseryman was listing twenty-six different fuchsias, some of which seem to have only been forms of *F. magellanica*, while others were hybrids. However, the fuchsia did not develop as we know it today until *F. fulgens* became generally available. This was first received in 1830, but does not seem to have been generally available before 1837, when, once more, Lee & Kennedy distributed plants. The modern *Fuchsia* has largely been developed from hybrids between *F. fulgens* and *F. magellanica*. A more or less albino form of *F. magellanica* known at the time as 'Rosea Alba' was the parent in the first white sepalled fuchsias 'Venus Victrix' and 'Enchantress' which appeared in the early 1840s and which formed the parents of a vast number of white-sepalled fuchsias bred by the nurseryman James Lye, which were raised in the 1870s.

The modern lupin was not available to the nineteenth-century gardener, although he had its chief ancestor, *L. polyphyllus*, which had been sent back by Douglas in 1826, though this was cultivated in a number of different colour forms. Although a large number of *Lupin* species have been introduced to English gardens, most of them have not been found easy to perpetuate and the only other lupin generally available in the early years of the century was *L. nootkatensis*. Whether anyone attempted to cross this with *L. polyphyllus* is unrecorded, but given the horticultural climate of the time it would seem probable.

A number of *Gladiolus* species had been available ever since Masson's collecting expeditions. Most of the early hybridisation was done among the smaller species, but the 'Colvillei' strain (raised ostensibly from *G. cardinalis* × *G. tristis*) dates from 1823. The tall, large-flowered, gladioli date from 1842 when growers in Belgium crossed *G. psittacinus* with *G. oppositiflorus* and also with *G. cardinalis*. The resulting strains were known as 'Gandavensis' and 'Antwerpensis', while a British counterpart was known as 'Brenchleyensis'. The strain of hybrid remained stationary for some forty years until, in the 1880s, Lemoine introduced mauve and lavender colours with *G. purpureo-auratus*

10 A rock garden in Scotland in the 1830s

11 Redleaf, near Penshurst. Rocks used for protecting tender plants, 1835

12 Redleaf: a rococo garden

13 The villa of the artist Nesfield in 1839. It looks very modern, but is really a development of the wilderness, brought right up to the house

and *G. papilio*. Slightly later, *G. saundersii, G. cruentus* and *G. quartinianus*, all large flowered, long-spiked species were bred in to the various hybrids, while finally *G. nebulicola* (*G. primulinus*) was used to give a dwarfer plant. The modern gladiolus really is comparatively recent, although hybrid gladioli had been extensively grown since 1842.

The various species of *Mimulus*, which were mainly introduced from Chile and from western N. America, were so extensively hybridised that it is doubtful if any pure species still exist in cultivation.

Verbena hybridisation started in 1837 and the modern verbena is the result of the interhybridising of *VV. platensis, peruviana, phlogiflora* and *incisa*. It was always popular as a bedding plant, but during the 1870s it was much improved by Henry Eckford and a large number of named cvs were available.

The modern delphinium is mainly derived from *D. elatlum*, a European plant which has been in cultivation since Gerard's day. Other species that were grown include *DD. cheilanthum* and *exaltatum*, and the modern delphinium is supposed to be derived mainly from these three species together with *D. formosum*, which has a tendency to produce white forms.

Maybe enough has been said to show the sudden astonishing number of different flowers that were suddenly available to the interested gardener, and it is not surprising that the garden was to become altered from a place where flowers were scantily treated to one where they received pre-eminence. Even before the flood of hybrids started the choice had become enormous. In the *Garden* for July 31st, 1880, is printed a list of the herbaceous plants grown by the rector of Bitton, H. T. Ellacombe (father of the famous Canon H. N. Ellacombe). This runs to over 2,000 species, although it does include ferns and aquatics, as well as various cultivars, and one has only to read the catalogues of such firms as Loddiges or Lee & Kennedy for the 1820s to realise the enormous choice that had suddenly become open to the plant grower.

These herbaceous lists also included a number of alpines. From Loddiges's catalogue of 1823 I can see three *Androsace* species, *Anemone baldensis* and *A. halleri*; *Anemonella thalictroides* (including the double form); *Anthyllis montana*;

Aquilegia alpina and *A. viridiflora*; nine *Arabis species;* thirteen
Arenaria species; *Aster alpinus;* sixteen *Astraglus* species; a
vast number of campanulas including *C.C. barbata, carpatica* and
thyrsoidea; *Cardamine asarifolia*; various alpine *Chrysanthemum* species; *Cortusa matthioli*; four *Cypripedium* species; five
Draba species; three *Epipactis* species; *Erodium chamaedryoides*;
Eryngium alpinum; *Dicentra cucullaria, D. eximia* and *D.
nobilis*; nineteen *Gentiana* species, including a number from N.
America; a number of *Geranium* species, *Habenaria fimbriata*
and *H. lacera*; a number of plants labelled helonias, but probably
including *Zigadenus*; four *Heuchera* species; a large number of
Iris species including *II. aphylla, cristata, graminea, ruthenica*
and many that cannot easily be identified; four *Lycopodium*
species; *Petrocallis pyrenaica*; a number of dwarf *Phlox* species;
nine *Phyteuma* species; *Plantago alpina*; numerous *Potentilla*
species; thirteen *Primula* species; twelve *Prunella* species; many
Ranunculus species including *RR. alpestris, amplexicaulis,
glacialis, gouanii, gramineus, parnassifolius, polyanthemos
(=Anemone narcissiflora?), rutaefolius* and *thora; Rubus
arcticus.* Remarkably there were sixty-five *Saxifraga* species
(including *Bergenia*); then several dwarf *Scabiosa* species;
Scutellaria alpina; twenty-seven *Sedum* species; nineteen *Silene*
species; three *Soldanella* species; several dwarf *Stachys*; thirty-
seven *Thalictrum* species, not all alpine but many not easy to
identify; four *Thymus* species; seventeen *Trifolium* species; six
Trollius species; forty-seven *Veronica* species; thirty-three *Viola*
species; four *Uvularia* species and *Wulfenia carinthiaca*. This,
remember, was in 1823 long before Douglas had sent back any
plants from western N. America. The number of herbaceous
plants listed runs into more than a thousand; although it contains many that would not be admitted to gardens nowadays, it
also probably includes many that we would be only too pleased
to see reintroduced. It is scarcely surprising that the flower
garden was completely transformed in the nineteenth century.

Finally, we should perhaps mention those nurserymen who
seem to have specialised in the cultivation of native plants, particularly in their abnormal variants. The most complete list
known to me occurs in Loudon's *Gardener's Magazine* for 1830
and includes a communication from the nurseryman himself, a

Mr. James Smith of Monkwood Grove near Ayr. This was apparently received in 1827, but the accompanying manuscript was so illegible that it took Loudon some time to decipher it. In a covering letter Mr. Smith claims credit for the diagnosis of *Primula scotica* and also says, 'I have sure information that *Soldanella alpina* is a native of Wales; please let me know if it is generally known as such.' I suppose this is not impossible; *Lloydia serotina* still exists in Snowdonia and A. D. Webster, in his book on British orchids seems to have found *Dactylorhiza majalis* in Wales. Possibly there was at one time a small population of *Soldanella*.

The following are some of the more extraordinary plants that James Smith lists: *Acer pseudoplatanus* with silver leaves, with yellow leaves, with variegated leaves. *Acer campestre* with variegated leaves. Horse chestnuts with silver and with gold variegation, with pink flowers. Alders with variegated leaves, oak-leaved and varieties termed *laciniata* and *grossulariaefolia*. *Arbutus unedo* with variegated leaves and with double flowers. A variegated birch; a variegated and pendulous box and one with very narrow leaves; variegated hornbeams and varieties named *quercifolia, asplenifolia* and *pendula*. Variegated sweet chestnuts and a form called 'Asplenifolia'; a variegated *Laburnum*; *Crataegus oxyacantha* with double flowers, with pink flowers, *fructu aureo, fructu luteo, fructu bicolori, fructu striato*, var *apetala* (described as beautiful, though it is not clear why), a variant with singular recurved thorns, and a variant with variegated shoots and leaves. A variegated dogwood, hazels with golden and with variegated leaves. *Daphne mezereum* with white fruit and a form known as 'Serotinum', which sounds intriguing. A large number of cvs of *Calluna vulgaris*. Spindle trees with variegated leaves and with white fruits. A number of ash variants including one with striped bark, one with variegated bark and leaves and one with golden bark and leaves. The wild privet with blotched leaves and with yellow fruits. A variegated *Pinus sylvestris* and various other variegated conifers of either *Abies* or *Picea* species. A bird cherry with variegated leaves and a double-flowered plum. A variegated oak, and also several with unusual leaves. Red and black currants with variegated leaves and a currant with laciniate leaves and green fruits. *Rosa arvensis* with variegated leaves and with double flowers, a double *Rosa canina*, ten single forms of *Rosa spinosissima*, one with variegated leaves, and over 100 double forms 'most of them of our own rearing, thirty-five of which are very fine'. There were double white and pink blackberries and ones with silver and with golden variegation and variegated plants of willows, elders, woody nightshade, rowan and *Vaccinium vitis-idaea*. There were Limes with fern-leaves, and with yellow bark. There was a pink guelder rose, as well as a variegated one, and even a variegated Gorse, besides the double form. This is only a selection of the more unusual shrubs and trees.

There is also a list of herbaceous plants, which contains fewer surprises, particularly if we except all the variegated-leaved forms. However there was *Anemone nemorosa* with pink, with blue and with double flowers, as well as a form Smith termed 'Grandiflora'. About sixty varieties of *Bellis perennis*, 'single, double and proliferous, many of them very fine'. Double forms of most of the British campanulas, a double form of *Cardamine pratensis* and of a white form of this. A double greater celandine, a double *Colchicum autumnale*, forms he calls 'Caerulea' and 'Versicolor' and, of course, one with variegated leaves. A lily-of-the-valley with double flowers and variegated leaves and a double Solomon's seal. A red form of *Calystegia sepium*. A double form of *Fritillaria meleagris* and of *Gentianella campestris*. Double forms of both the blue and white *Geranium pratense* and numerous albino forms of other species. Double forms of *Hesperis matronalis* and a form with single, blotched flowers. Variegated forms of *Iris pseudacorus* and *I. foetidissima*. There were various double forms of *Silene* species. Double forms of *Ranunculus bulbosus*, *R. acris*, *R. ficaria* and *R. repens*, while there was also a white form of the common celandine. Of the devil's bit scabious selection there were white and red forms, white and red forms of *Scilla verna* and of the bluebell and a number of variants of the hart's tongue fern. The double *Silene maritima*, the variegated *Sedum acre*, double forms of meadow sweet and of *Filipendula vulgaris*, a white form of *Trollius europaeus* and double forms of *Viola odorata*, as well as white and red forms, which were both single and double.

The rest of his plants are either albinos or have variegated leaves. I think you will agree that this would have been an impressive list at any time and the date of 1827 shows more eloquently than any statistics how absorbed in gardening the British must have become. There are one or two curiosities. I suppose the variegated ground elder could not have been resisted, but ten peculiar plantains seems a lot and the list ends with the stinging nettle, either to be sold according to sex or, as a great rarity, a hermaphrodite form. Incidentally, has anyone seen an albino form of *Pulmonaria officinalis* recently?

These lists may seem a little tedious, but now that we know what material was available to the gardeners, we can go on to consider how they used it.

6

The Nineteenth Century:
Part 1

As the century opened, the dominant figure in landscape gardening was Repton, who was pursuing the 'natural' and 'picturesque' methods of which Brown is perhaps the main exponent. He was intelligent enough to know that painting and landscaping were not identical; a point that seems obvious enough, but a fallacy to which many gardeners were to fail to appreciate from the days of Uvedale Price to our own century. Even Repton himself does not seem to have been entirely immune from the confusion. There is a famous drawing of his own garden in which the view of the butcher's shop opposite is obscured by a pyramid of climbing roses, but a moment's thought will show that a few paces to the right or to the left would reveal the offending sight once more.

If one is going to equate garden design with the visual arts, it would seem that sculpture would prove a better model. A sculpture is, after all, three-dimensional, and one can walk round it and view it from different directions, but even this parallel cannot be pushed too far. A garden is a living thing, changing with the seasons; plants grow and plants die; the twig of today may be a sturdy sapling in seven years and a fine tree in fifteen, while the sculpture remains static for all time. Garden design is not to be equated with the visual arts; there are too many imponderables.

It has so happened that the flower garden has empirically been designed over the course of the years in order to show a number of constant features, most of which we have already seen

adumbrated by writers from Bacon onwards. The main difference is that before the nineteenth century flowers were a minor
detail in garden design, but subsequently they became of the
greatest importance. However, like everything else, there were
reactions to the prevailing trends. At one moment the bedding
system, where beds were filled with brilliant flowers, was
universally accepted. Then came the reaction. The private
gardeners returned to growing hardy plants, in place of the
bedding plants which needed glass protection in winter, while
even in public places, where some form of conspicuous work was
essential, flower bedding was superseded by the so-called subtropical bedding. In this, the interest lay not in flowers, but in
foliage and the sudden enthusiasm for massive and for coloured
foliage is one of the least expected characteristics of the later
nineteenth century.

Another feature of the century was the growth of specialisa-
tion. The old wilderness was separated into shrubbery on the one
hand and fernery on the other. The old rockwork eventually
became the alpine garden and there was a development of the
old private botanic garden into pinetuams, salicetums, rose gardens and other compartments dedicated to a single genus. The
removal of the tax on sheet glass in 1845 meant that greenhouses
were available to the middle classes, while improved boilers and
cheap transport of fuel also encouraged the growth of tender
plants. Grand houses such as Chatsworth not only rivalled, but
even outshone Kew in the earlier years of the century, while a
rich lady, Mrs. Lawrence of Ealing Park was growing and
exhibiting plants that no one else would even have obtained. Mr.
Wilson Saunders of Reigate was able to finance the sending of a
collector to South Africa. All the main nurserymen employed
collectors in the tropics, but the importation of hardy plants
was barely encouraged, until towards the end of the century
Regel and Sintenis explored the Near East and brought back
many tulips and iris. Also towards the end of the century, as we
have seen, the Far East began to yield its apparently endless
wealth of hardy flowers. The Royal Horticultural Society had
encouraged the collection of hardy plants, but after Fortune's
first journey to China their finances became so confused that no
further collectors could be sent.

To start with we can consider what might be regarded as the basic outlook towards flower gardening in the early years of the century. Here is part of an article written by Patrick Neill for the seventh edition of the *Encyclopaedia Britannica*, which was published separately in 1838.

'The designing of flower gardens unquestionably belongs to the fine arts, involving in it the exercise of invention, taste and foresight. Its principals are more vague and evanescent than those of any of the sister arts. The hand of the designer is not here guided by the imitation of Nature, for his work is wholly artificial in its arrangements and appliances; neither does utility come in, as in architecture, to supply a form and framework, which it is the artist's part to adorn.'

'As flower gardens,' says Mr. Loudon, the best authority on this topic, 'are objects of pleasure, the principal which must serve as a guide in laying them out must be taste. Now in flower gardens, as in other objects, there are different kinds of tastes; these embodied are called styles or characters; and the great art of the designer is, having fixed on a style, to follow it out unmixed with other styles, or with any deviation which would interfere with the kind of taste or impression which that style is calculated to produce . . . As objects of fancy and taste the style of flower gardens are various. The modern style is a collection of irregular groups and masses, placed about the house as a medium, uniting it with the open lawn. The ancient geometric style, in place of irregular groups, employed symmetrical forms: in France adding statues and fountains; in Holland cut trees and grassy slopes; and in Italy, stone walls, walled terraces and flights of steps. In some situations these characteristics of parterres may, with propriety, be added to, or used instead of the modern sort, especially in flat situations; such as are inclosed by high walls; in towns, or where the principal building or object is in a style of architecture which will not render these appendages incongruous. There are other characters of gardens, such as the Chinese, which are not widely different from the modern; the Indian, which consists chiefly of walks under shade in squares of grass; the Turkish, which abounds in shady retreats, boudoirs of roses and aromatic herbs; and the Spanish, which is distinguished by trellis-work and fountains; but these gardens are not generally adapted to this climate, though, from contemplating and selecting what is beautiful or suitable in each, a style of decoration for the immediate vicinity of mansions, might be composed preferable to anything now in use.

'It may, however, be remarked, that the flower garden, properly so-called, has generally been too much governed by the laws of landscape gardening, and these often ill-understood and misapplied. In the days of "clipped hedges and pleached alleys", the parterres and flower beds were of a description the most grotesque and intricate imaginable. At a subsequent period, when the natural and picturesque became the objects of limitation in the park, there appeared the most extravagant attempts of wildness in the garden. The result has been equally unfortunate. It is not meant that when there are merely a few patches of flowers by way of foreground to the lawn, they should not be subordinated to the principles which regulate the more distant and bolder scenery; but wherever there is a flower garden of considerable magnitude, and in a separate situation, we think it should be constructed on principles of its own. In such a spot, the great object must be to exhibit, to advantage, the graceful forms and glorious hues of flowering plants and shrubs; and it is seldom that mere elegancies in the forms of compartments and other trickeries of human invention, can bear any comparison with these natural beauties. To express the peculiar nature of garden scenery, as distinct from the picturesque in landscape, Mr. Loudon has invented the term *Gardenesque*; and, whatever may be thought of the term itself, it is very desirable that the distinction should be preserved.

'Two varieties of flower gardens have chiefly prevailed in Britain; one in which the ground is turf, and the pattern, so to speak, is composed of a variety of figures cut out of the turf, and planted with flowers and shrubs; and another, when the flower beds are separated by gravel walks, without being dispersed by grass at all. The choice of one or other of these varieties ought greatly to depend upon the situation. When the flower garden is to be seen from the windows, or any other elevated point of view, from which the whole or the greater part of the design may be perceived at once, perhaps the former should be preferred. Where the surface is irregular, and the situation more remote, and

especially where the beauty of flowers is the chief object of con-
templation, the choice should probably fall on the latter. This
variety, too, seems preferable, on the principle of contrast, where
there are large lawns in the outer grounds, in order that kept (or
smoothly mown) grass may not be found everywhere.

'Respecting the situation of the flower garden, no very precise
directions can be given, as it must be influenced by the size of
the domain, the nature of the lawns and the site of the mansion,
to which it is attached. Generally speaking it should not be at
any great distance from the house; and in places where there is
no distant view of importance, it may be constructed under the
windows . . . On the other hand, when the park is spacious and
the prospects extensive, it is perhaps better that the flower garden
should be at some distance, but not more than a quarter of a mile
out of sight of the house, and with an easy access in any sort of
weather; an arrangement which should give an agreeable
termination to a short walk, a desirable matter in most cases, for
it has often been remarked that many parts of extensive grounds
remain unvisited, because they afford no remarkable object to
attract the attention.

'The particular form of a flower garden is equally beyond the
inculcation of specific rules. Indeed, it may be of any shape, and,
except where the dimensions are extremely limited, the
boundaries should not be continuously visible . . . By judicious
management it may be made to pass through shrubbery,
gradually assuming a more woodland character, and groups of
trees, into the park on the one hand and into the kitchen garden
or orchard on the other.

'A north wall of moderate extent and moderate elevation is
often desirable as affording space for ornamental climbers, and
half acclimatised exotics, and as forming a *point d'appui* for the
conservatory and other botanical structures. Such a wall may be
surmounted by urns and other architectural ornaments, and
screened at some little distance behind by trees. The other fences
may be of wire-work, generally called *invisible*, or of wooden
rails, or of holly hedges with rails.

'Formerly the flower beds were made either circular, straight,
or in curves and were turned into knots, scrolls, volutes, and
other compartments; and this taste prevailed, perhaps, in some

measure from a desire on the part of the contrivers, to compensate by their ingenuity for the paucity of the ornamental plants which they then cultivated. Now that the riches of Flora have poured into our gardens, a simpler taste has obtained. Of the figures in fashion at present in the lawn flower garden, perhaps the kidney shape and its varieties occur too frequently. It is needless as well as impossible to specify the numerous configurations of flower-pots, for they abound in kaleidoscopical variety. Good taste will suggest that those only should be associated, which harmonize well together; and it is better to incur the hazard of apparent monotony, than to excite wonder by incongruous combination. When the figures are separated by turf, it is necessary that the little lawns or glades should have a considerable degree of breadth, as nothing has a worse effect than over-crowding. A multitude of little figures should also be avoided, as they produce ... *spottiness* ... which ... is a grievous deformity. In this sort of flower garden it is desirable that a gravel walk should skirt along at least one side of the principal figures; in our humid climate, the grass would otherwise render them inaccessible with comfort during a great part of the year. In those gardens from which turf is excluded, the compartments should be of a larger and more massive character. Narrow borders bounded by parallel straight lines and concentric curves should be avoided. The centres of the figures should be occupied with tall growing shrubs, and even with an occasional low evergreen tree, such as a yew or a holly. The walks, arranged in long concave curves, may communicate here and there with one another. A dial, a few seats and arbours, with an urn or two or a vase may be introduced with good effect. It is to be regretted that so few good specimens of this species of flower garden have hitherto been executed in Britain.

'Amongst the accompaniments of the flower garden may be mentioned the rock-work. This consists of variously grouped masses of large stones, generally such as are remarkable for being figured by water-wearing, or for containing petrifactions or impressions; and into the cavities between the stones, filled with earth, alpine, or trailing plants are inserted. These are numerous and may be endlessly diversified. Several species of Helianthemum, Gentiana, Pentstemon and Primula, Campanula pumila, blue and white varieties, carpatica and nitida; Saponaria ocymoides and Adonis vernalis may be recommended. In proper situations, a small piece of water may be introduced for the culture of aquatic plants. One of the walks is sometimes arched over with wire-work, and covered with ornamental climbing shrubs, forming a delightful promenade in the glowing days of summer. A separate compartment, generally of some regular figure, is set apart for roses. A moist, or rather shady border with bog earth, is devoted to that class of shrubs, commonly, but not very accurately, designated "American plants". In extensive places a separate "American garden" is often formed in a locality, which, if not damp, has at least the command of water, occupying generally some warm corner of the park.

'Some writers have advocated the formation of winter and spring gardens in separate localities; but we are not aware that their ideas have ever been embodied to any great extent. It is proposed that in the winter garden should be assembled all the hardy evergreen shrubs and plants together with a few flowers that bloom during the winter months. The situation, it is recommended, should be well sheltered and open only to the warm rays of the sun, which are peculiarly grateful in our cold brumal seasons. However attractive this scheme may be in theory, it seems doubtful whether it would be very successful in execution. Masses of evergreen have a sombre and monotonous effect, even in winter, unless occasionally broken and varied by deciduous trees. The contrast of their leafless neighbours relieves the intenseness of their gloom and sets off their brilliancy. Though a winter garden, the very name of which is chilling, is perhaps not very desirable in itself, the object to be attained in it should be kept in view . . . We can easily suppose a particular section . . . to contain a predominance of evergreens and to possess the principal characters of a winter garden, without the formality of its name and purpose . . . Again the spring garden, which need not be of very great extent, may take refuge in the vicinity of the greenhouse or conservatory, with which it is naturally allied.'

There are two remarkable things about this article. Firstly, if I may use a Sherlockismus, it is remarkable because it is so unremarkable; it could go practically unaltered into any contemporary book on garden layout. Admittedly, there are few gardens nowadays where a walk of not more than a quarter of a mile can be recommended with much confidence, but the general principles are still unexceptionable. The other remarkable quality is that the article had already become out-of-date. Slowly, the flower garden was returning to the formal geometric style of the seventeenth century and this trend was to persist for some time.

During the years of its publication, Loudon's *Gardener's Magazine* was thought of as particularly up-to-date with regard to all things pertaining to the craft from machinery and methods of heating greenhouses to plants and garden design. On page 424 of the volume for the year 1830 is a design for a flower garden, which is of formal and geometric design, although the symmetry is not entirely insisted upon. It was apparently designed by 'a young lady'. The plan is on a scale of 16 ft. to the inch so, that the garden may be expected to be about 120 ft. long and 50 ft. broad – a fairly typical back-yard in dimensions.

Besides the design we also have a planting plan and, at the risk of more plant listing, it is perhaps worth looking at this. As can be seen, the original plan is rectangular, but an elliptic effect is given by the planting of the shrubs around the margin. These are said to be early-flowering deciduous specimens, and low or slow-growing evergreens; the great object being to admit sufficient sun and air, 'without which the flowers come to nothing'.

If we start from near the scale, the whole of the part before the beds and borders begin is of gravel, with a covered rustic seat in the centre, and a 'rustic arcade covered with ivy' on either side of this. Between the gravel and the shrub edging are two small pieces of rockwork, presumably mounded. These appear to be 16 ft. long but only 4 ft. across at the widest point. Within the shrub edging, and forming the margin of the ellipse, there is an edging of *Rosa semperflorens* (presumably *R. chinensis*), while behind are dahlias in 100 different varieties, with a standard Noisette rose planted every 12 ft.

The beds are all set in lawn. In the centre is a sundial, while the beds surrounding this are planted alternatively with anemones or with Van Thol tulips and ranunculi in spring; and with tigridias and choice dwarf geraniums in summer. The rather amorphously-shaped bed between the sun-dial and the rustic seat is planted with choice herbaceous perennials, while complementing this, beyond the dial, is a crown-shaped bed that is planted with 'Narcissus and Jonquils in spring; Salvia splendens and Fuchsia coccinea in summer'. The two narrow beds between the sun-dial and the larger, comma-shaped beds were planted with ten-week stocks in spring and *Clarkia* and *Dianthus chinensis* in summer. The comma-shaped beds were planted with sweet-scented and crimson China roses. Beyond these, on the left of the plan, the tadpole-shaped bed was planted with *Fritillaria meleagris* and winter aconite in spring; *Lobelia fulgens* and *L. erinus* in summer, while the matching bed on the right had hyacinths in spring and *Fuchsia macrophylla* (?) in summer. At the top of the plan, on either side of the crown-shaped bed, were a pair of beds with tulips in spring and *Oenothera speciosa* in summer. Flanking these beds are a pair of sausage-shaped compartments, of which the one on the left contained a collection of campanulas, while that on the right contained a collection of phlox.

Finally, back to the front of the garden; the two S-shaped beds on either side of the large herbaceous bed were planted with snowdrops and crocuses in spring, carnations and pinks in summer, while the axe-head shaped beds beyond them contained, on the left, choice herbaceous plants, while on the right were *Oenothera* and China asters.

It is not, we must confess, a labour-saving garden, and one or two of the proposed arrangements appear slightly strange. *Lobelia erinus* is the small, blue, creeping *Lobelia* that was later to be so widely used in bedding schemes and might have seemed a trifle garish as an underplanting to the scarlet *L. fulgens*. More mysterious is the mention of 'Choice dwarf Geraniums'. These would not be the compact bedding scarlet ones as they had not yet been bred; the most famous of these, 'Tom Thumb', did not enter into commerce before 1844. I suspect that what are referred to here are the Unique and Pet strains bred from crossing Regal pelargoniums with the scented-leaved species and hybrids. In those days the scarlet geraniums, as we shall see, were tall, shrubby plants. Another odd feature is the planting of ten-week stocks as a spring subject. Presumably they were treated like wallflowers – sown in July and planted out in the autumn.

This garden was fairly geometric, but simplicity itself compared to what was to appear in pages of the magazine in its latter numbers. On pages 167 onwards for the last volume to be published in 1843, Loudon himself published his thoughts on 'Laying out and Planting the Lawn, Shrubbery and Flower Garden'. The article is too long to reproduce in full, although one must endeavour to give a precis. What I wish to consider here is the plan for An Architectural Flower-Garden, which appears on page 173. We learn that it was designed for a particular situation at Bitteswell in Leicestershire. The beds were supposed to have stone edgings, while the interstices were paved. The central diamond was a fountain, while the two circles were of grass with a pedestal and statue in the centre. The little square beds at the corners, and at the centre edge, held large vases. Loudon then sent the plan to four eminent gardeners to submit lists of how the garden should be planted. Philip Frost of Dropmore Gardens was principally interested in the summer display, although he noted that beds to be planted with such things as pelargoniums, could have tulips to start with. All the beds, incidentally, are only 3 ft. wide. His list included some unusual plants, such as *Isotoma axillaris*, *Nolana atripliciflora*, *Alonsoa linearis* and *A. incisifolia*. He also had Cooper's 'Dwarf Scarlet' *Pelargonium*, which must have been a precursor of 'Tom Thumb'. Mr. Caie of Bedford Lodge produced two lists. The first gave flowers from early spring until June; the second those from June onwards. The first list contains some very interesting plants such as various dwarf *Phlox* species; *Sanguinaria canadensis* (an unusual choice for a bedding plant); *Iris verna*, *Corydalis nobilis*; *Dielytra formosa*; *Galanthus plicatus* and *Lilium longiflorum*. What can this last plant have been? The summer list is mainly composed of *Petunia*, *Verbena*, *pelargoniums*, including ivy-leaved ones, but includes *Tournefortia heliotropioides*, a form of scentless but showy heliotrope.

Mr. Pringle of Duncombe Park also submitted two lists; the latter for the use of those who had not much glass to work with. But both lists were so arranged that summer flowers would follow spring ones without the need to replant the beds completely. For example, there would be an edging of striped crocus, while within would be four standard roses underplanted with French marigolds. In his second list the same bed retained its edging of striped crocuses, but within were various species of *Phlox*. Not all the beds were as straightforward as this, and a number had roses trained on 'a flat terrace'. I suppose that means that they were tied to a horizontal, rather than a vertical trellis to keep them compact. Mr. Pringle liked American plants and three beds were composed of *Gaulteria shallon*, yellow azaleas, *Gaultheria procumbens* and red azaleas and vacciniums of different species; besides these there were beds of rhododendrons and andromedas.

Finally, Mr. W. P. Ayres of Acton submitted no less than three lists: the first was of spring bulbs which, as soon as they had finished, were to be whipped out and replaced by summer-flowering annuals, which were, in turn, to be supplanted chiefly by greenhouse plants for an autumn display. The annuals included *Clintonia pulchella*; *Schizopetalon walkeri*; various *Gilia* species (some as *Leptosiphon*); *Collinsia verna* and *C. bicolor* and various *Godetia* species. Among the autumnal plants were some unexpected species such as *Crucianella stylosa*; *Lobelia (Isotoma) axillaris; Nierembergia filicaulis* and *N. intermedia*, and numerous verbenas, pelargoniums, calceolarias and petunias.

Inspired by this result, Loudon sent out other designs with suggested plantings, which can be found on pages 261 *ff.* in the 1843 volume. It looks as though this might have turned into a form of competition. We can see that it is only a short step from these geometric gardens to the bedding system that was to generate such high feelings in the next decade. However, for the moment, let us return to the article in which the original design was first shown.

'The principles,' Loudon starts off by saying, 'which serve to guide us in laying out the details of a place are derived from its natural and artificial character, and the wants and wishes of the proprietor.' He then deals with a knotty point and one that few garden designers allude to. He says that the wishes of the proprietor should be acceded to 'except in the case of what the artist considers bad taste. In this case he must respectfully . . . argue the matter with his employer. Should he fail in producing the conviction desired, it will be a question for him to resolve how far he can, consistently with his own reputation, sanction the production of what he considers in bad taste; at the same time carefully distinguishing between taste which is inherently bad, and taste which is merely peculiar. For example, suppose an employer wished to terminate a vista with a landscape painted on canvas; or to introduce in a verdant scene, a flat surface of boards painted so as to resemble a rock or a cottage? This taste, except in the garden of a *guingette,* we should consider as radically bad . . .

'Bearing these data in view, there are three styles or systems of art according to which lawns and shrubberies may be laid out. The first of these is the *geometric style,* characterised by lines which require to be drawn geometrically . . .; the second is the *picturesque style,* characterised by that irregularity in forms, lines and general composition, which we see in natural land-scape; and the third is the *gardenesque* style, characterised by distinctness in the separate parts when closely examined, but, when viewed as a whole, governed by the same general principles of composition as the picturesque style, the parts, though not blended, being yet connected.' This may seem slightly obscure, but is explained later:

'The geometric style admits of several varieties, according to the prevailing features. In one case architectural objects, such as stone edgings to beds, stone terraces . . . may be prevalent and this will constitute the architectural style. In another, statues, vases and other sculptural objects may be frequent . . . and con-stitute, of course, the sculpturesque style. Where the trees and shrubs are for the most part cut into artificial shapes . . . the result is the tonsile style, or verdant sculpturesque. Where stone terraces, terrace gardens and sculpture are combined, the result is the Italian style; and grass terraces, turf mounts and straight canals constitute the Dutch style.

'The picturesque style varies according to the natural character of the surface, and the kind of art employed. It may be the hilly, the rocky, the aquatic, the trivial or common, or the elegant or refined, picturesque . . . The elegant or refined picturesque is exemplified in lawns and pleasure grounds, where the surface has been reduced to smooth undulations, levels or slopes, and where the trees and shrubs grouped on these surfaces are of exotic species, or of such varieties of the common kind as are not frequently to be met with. Other varieties of the picturesque, resulting from rocks, water, &c., will readily occur to the reader.

'The gardenesque style is to gardening, as an art of culture, what the picturesque style is to landscape-painting, as an art of design and taste. All the trees, shrubs and plants in the gardenesque style are planted and managed in such a way as that each may arrive at perfection and display its beauties to as great advantage as if it were cultivated for that purpose alone; while at the same time, the plants relatively to one another and to the whole scene . . . are either grouped or connected on the same principals of composition as in the picturesque style, or placed regularly and symmetrically as in the geometric style. Hence there are two distinct varieties . . . the geometric gardenesque and the pictorial gardenesque; . . .

'Two or more of these styles may be employed in the same pleasure-ground, but not indiscriminately mixed there. When more than one style is employed, it can only be done with good effect by using the styles in succession . . . For example, the Italian style may prevail on the lawn front of the house, and may lose itself in grass terraces of the Dutch style; beyond which may be exhibited, first the gardenesque, and then the picturesque; but to introduce alternatively portions of geometric or tonsile scenery with picturesque scenery would distract attention, and be destructive of that first of all principles in composition, the unity of the whole, which can only be produced by the connexion and harmony of the parts.'

We do not seem to have progressed in any way since that was written and it is not easy to see how we can. I imagine the bedding system, which was just around the corner when Loudon was writing, would be described by him as geometric gardenesque, while this has since been supplanted by the pictorial gardenesque, which is still the prevalent style, although the confined spaces of modern gardens are inducing a return to the architectural style and I suppose the modern patio may claim to have introduced a Spanish note into gardens. However this may not be particularly novel. The construction of parts of the garden to resemble foreign parts was apparently quite common practice in the 1840s as the following extract from an article by 'A North Briton' from the *Floricultural Magazine* for 1841 (pages 134–5) would seem to indicate:

'Neat resting places should be placed in different parts, choosing the situation of some in shaded groves, others upon elevated spots . . . Much taste may be displayed in the formation of such seats, from the polished temple of Flora, Venus, &c., to the rude roots of trees and misshaped fragments of rocks or rude stone . . . Moss houses of various construction, root-houses, Russian, Swedish, Lapland, Scotch and Swiss cottages should be disposed of in situations peculiarly adapted for them. Sometimes situations are naturally to be found adapted for the one or the other; in such cases the house should be chosen to suit the situation . . . Where the situation has to be formed . . . much judgment and taste are required in the arrangement: this is not sufficiently attended to: thus a Russian cottage composed of oak timber trees, and the adjacent ground planted with laurel and other polished shrubs, natives of southern latitudes, and close-shaven grass lawns, is as preposterous as the chaste Grecian temple in a rocky dingle. The ground should be chosen or arranged so as to persuade the observer that he really is in Russia, and the house should be composed of the same timber-trees used in the formation of cottages in that country, and be of the same form and size . . . Hermitages and caves are also interesting when proper situations are chosen: in these could be kept a small collection of books calculated for private study, and the furniture of this sequestered retreat should be exactly of that simple and useful nature as would be suitable to a recluse.'

Our 'North Briton' does not mention Spanish or Portuguese imitations, but there would obviously be no objections to the idea.

The above extract comes, surprisingly, from an article entitled 'On the Formation of Shrubberies', but after the flower garden this was an object of most interest to the gardeners of the nineteenth century. Since the Victorian shrubbery has been an object of almost universal condemnation we should perhaps examine the principles which lay at its conception and construction and, to start with, we may well stay with our builder of Swiss cottages.

'The shrubbery may be defined to be the link which connects the mansion and the lawn to the flower garden, or to the other parts of a residence, and is most generally planted either for shelter or shade, although often as a screen to hide disagreeable objects, for which the plants that compose it are better suited than for forest or other trees. The shrubbery is often a matter of utility as well as of ornament.' This would appear to have been the basic conception, but there were exceptions:

'Sometimes a shrubbery is formed merely for the purpose of growing rare shrubs, and for obtaining agreeable walks; in this case it is necessary to be at more pains, and to display a greater degree of taste in the laying of it out . . .'

This is, of course, the modern shrub garden of today; a form that was to become increasingly popular as more ornamental shrubs became available, but which was evidently somewhat unusual in 1840.

'In planting shrubberies for screens to hide disagreeable objects, evergreens should form the principal mass, as affording a permanent blind and giving a cheerful appearance even in winter. A few deciduous shrubs of the most showy sorts may, however, be with propriety added, which will give some relief to the more sombre appearance of the evergreens, particularly while the former are in flower . . .

'In the disposal of the shrubs the tallest should be planted farthest from the walk or front side, and the lower in stature in front, but if an immediate effect be desired it is better to elevate the ground than to plant trees of too great an age; it is also a matter of importance that they may be planted thickly, as it is an easy task to thin them out when required.'

I would like to pause at this last sentence, as it demonstrates a gardening fallacy which has existed from the clumps of Capability Brown to the present day. In theory, it is always easy to thin out plantings that are too thick, but in practice gardeners are extremely loath to do this and, in any case, through having been planted too thickly originally, the shrubs tend to be leggy and misshapen. One reason for the bad reputation of the

Victorian shrubbery owed itself to the fact that the intended subsequent thinning out was never attended to. As we have seen this was not intentional.

Let us return to our 'North Briton':

'Great attention should be paid . . . to give them a somewhat natural appearance, and not that of a surface as regular as if it were clipped with the garden shears. Straight lines should be avoided as much as possible, and the margin of the shrubbery should be broken with deep indentures and sinuosities . . . The walks which lead through this department should not be to any great distance in a straight line if it can be avoided, neither should they be too much twisted. There is something in a fine gentle sweep or curve so pleasing in a road or walk, that few are insensible of its beauty. The breadth of the walks should be regulated according to the length and scale of the place, as too narrow walks . . . have never a good effect; they should scarcely, under any circumstances, be less than five feet wide and unless for terrace walks of great length should not be more than eight . . .'

It all sounds very familiar, and in how many gardens can we still see today the shrubberies recommended by our author?

There were, however, other writers who were considering the shrubbery with more subtlety – following on the thoughts already enunciated by Peter Collinson and anticipating the artistic tenets of Gertrude Jekyll. In 1838, the Rev. Henry Hill was writing (*Floricultural Cabinet*, 1838, p. 86.)

'One of the most important things in planting is to attend particularly to the shades of green, especially where the view from the house or lawn catches the trees. Flowers . . . continue but for a short period in comparison to the duration of foliage; therefore the picture should be formed by judiciously contrasting the greens. Even the effect of perspective may be considerably increased by the proper arrangement of hues. [This had already been adumbrated by Shenstone in his famous garden of the Leasowes in the mid-eighteenth century.] Trees whose leaves are grey or bluish tint, when seen over or between shrubs of a yellow or bright green seem to be thrown into the distance. Trees with small and tremulous leaves should wave over or before those of broad or fixed foliage. The light and elegant acacia has a more beautiful effect when its branches float over the firm and dark holly or bay tree. In some situations the bare trunk of trees may be shown; in some it should be concealed by evergreens and creepers. Vines, also, may be suffered to embrace it and form natural festoons where the extent of the ground will allow of wilderness scenery. In all situations nature may be assisted, but should never be deformed . . .'

He, also, has something to say about overcrowding.

'The beauty of plants cannot be displayed when they are too much crowded, as they are then drawn up into unnatural shapes. Therefore, the oftener open spaces can be admitted, the more will the shrubs exhibit themselves to advantage, and the more cheerful will be the walk; for it becomes insipid and gloomy when confined for any distance.' This clergyman did not like the formal garden: 'Bad taste is seldom more conspicuous than when we see trees or plants marshalled in regular order and at equal distances, like beaux and belles standing up for a quadrille or country dance. Where the situation will permit four or six lilacs sould be grouped in one place, and as many laburnums in another so as to give effect in various parts by a mass of colour. The guelder rose should appear as if escaping from the dark bosom of evergreens, and not a plant should be set in the ground without adding to the harmony of the whole. A shrubbery should be planted, as a court or stage dress is ornamented, for general effect, and not particular and partial inspection. Boldness of design, which seems to be more the offspring of nature and chance than of art and study should be attempted; but . . . all harshness or too great abruptness should be avoided by a judicious mixture of plants whose colours will blend easily into one another.'

The language alters somewhat as year succeeds year, but the sentiments are remarkably constant. Henry Hill seems to have thought the whole matter out very thoroughly:

'A well planted shrubbery depends not so much for its beauty on the expense and rarity of the plants it contains, as on the selection of trees and shrubs which succeed each other in blossoming throughout the year, or whose various-coloured fruits grace them for the longest duration of time.' Although he recommends variegated evergreens to give attraction in winter, he does not seem to have paid any attention to autumn tints. However, I may be misjudging him as his thoughts on the autumnal shrubbery were for some reason not printed, despite of the superb introductory paragraph.

'To those who are so devoted to fashion, as not to venture to treat their lungs with air, unmixed with smoke, till the crowds that swarmed at court have fixed their departure for rural scenes and a pure atmosphere, like swallows and other birds of passage; to such the gaiety of the autumnal shrubbery is of most importance. It remains to say how the last expiring ray of beauty may be thrown over the pleasure-ground.' Alas, as far as the *Floricultural Cabinet* is concerned, the series of articles breaks off at this point.

The fact that the garden had become a place for flowers, rather than for trees and water, necessitated the conception of new principles in laying out the garden. These were, perhaps, best illustrated by the foremost theorist of the day, J. C. Loudon in 1840. (*Gardener's Magazine*, pages 620 *ff.*) He begins by insisting on the axis of symmetry, which he explains thus:

'The axis of symmetry is founded on this principle: that all the most beautiful objects or scenes in nature are symmetrical; that every symmetrical object forms a whole; and that every whole consists of at least three parts, a beginning, a middle and an end; or, in other words, a centre and two sides. Now, in this centre, whether visible or supplied by the imagination is the axis of symmetry. In the simplest kind of symmetry, the two sides are equal and alike, and the axis is, of course, easily discovered; but in cultivated and refined symmetry, the sides are unequal, and so combined and varied with the centre, that it requires the eye of a philosophical artist to detect the axis; which, in other words, is called the axis of composition . . . But, though every artist will allow this to be theoretically true, yet he will also allow that it requires great practical experience to be able to carry the idea into effect, especially in general scenery. In the case of a house . . . the difficulty is not great . . . but in landscape all the forms are indefinite, and continually changing by growth, by decay, and even by the seasons of the year. Those who have thought much on this subject will discover that the idea of rendering every object or scene symmetrical is but a more accurate and detailed analysis of the expression, "rendering any object or scene a whole". The advantage of treating the subject in this manner is like that of presenting the same object under different points of view; we become better acquainted with it.'

Louden then goes into a few details, beginning with Breadth of Effect. 'Without it, that is in common language, without broad naked surfaces or glades of turf among trees and shrubs, there must either be monotony or confusion . . . The use of these naked places in parks and pleasure grounds is to contrast with the covered places; because it is by this contrast that what is called the effect is produced. In other words, a thing is what it is only by comparison with some other thing . . . In short there is not a principle of composition . . . of landscape gardening . . . so constantly brought into requisition as that of contrast, unless, indeed, it be that of connexion. The whole art of landscape gardening . . . with reference to effect, may, indeed, be resolved into the exercise of these two principles.'

Loudon now turns to more practical details, particularly to the shape of beds. Beds, the outlines of which form acute angles, are bad in themselves, in his eyes, 'because they can never be completely covered with flowers or shrubs at the angles, and because, if the eye of the spectator . . . is not on a much higher level, the shape of the bed . . . is not recognised. For all ordinary purposes therefore, we consider acute-angled beds as ineligible; though for symmetrical designs, in situations where the design is commanded by elevated walk or surrounding terrace, they may with propriety be introduced; because in such situations their forms and combinations display them to almost all the advantage of which they are susceptible.

'We wish we could strongly impress on the mind of every amateur and of every gardener, that for all practical purposes of planting beds of shrubs or beds of flowers on a lawn, to be laid out in the modern style, the best form is the circle, provided that it be always kept of small size, say from 18 in. to 6 ft. in diameter, one circle never to be placed nearer to another than 2 ft., and that these beds be thrown together in groups and constellations, as stars are in the firmament, or single trees and single shrubs in a well planted park . . .

'Some persons who do not understand the difference between the effects of shapes on paper and shapes on ground, and between looking down on a lawn or flower garden and looking at it sideways, will object to having nothing but circles as wanting in variety; but in practice it is found that, by combinations of circles of different sizes, more variety is produced than can be effected by the use of any other form whatever . . . To show that combinations of circles are productive of more variety than any other form, we may observe, first, that the circles being always seen from the side of the combination, change their apparent position with every change in the position of the spectator; and, secondly, that when the circles are planted with flowers, one or more of which in every bed rise to the height of 2 or 3 ft., the shape of the bed, whatever it may be, can never be recognised by the spectator from a side view. The size and connexion, therefore, in this case, is of much more importance than the shape. As well might combinations of single trees be objected to in a park, as combinations of small circular beds on a lawn; for, as a single tree, in combination with other single trees, is no longer a detached object, but forms a part of the whole to which it belongs, so a single circular bed, in combination with other circular beds, is no longer to be considered as a circle, but as the element of a combination which may form a varied and extensive figure, according to the circumstances of the situation and the object in view.

'The only fear that we have in recommending circles so strongly is, lest our doing so, should revive the old system of clumping in parks; but we hope it will always be borne in mind that we recommend no circles larger than 5 or 6 ft. in diameter, and none to be placed in such an isolated position as to be unconnected with anything else, and to attract attention as single and detached objects.'

The beds sometimes got larger and they were by no means invariably circular, but here is the English flower garden as we know it. This progress, however, was about to be stopped, and a reversion to formal gardening was to come in with the bedding system, which deserves a chapter to itself.

—7—
The Nineteenth Century:
Part 2

ONE CANNOT really give a definite date for the start of the bedding system, but 1845 is a convenient pivot. It was in this year that the tax on glass was removed, with the result that the building of greenhouses became much cheaper. Sheet glass had been first made in 1833 and then cost 1s. 2d. a foot. After 1845 this fell to 2d. The industrial revolution had also made the introduction of wrought iron a feasibility, so that heating could also be managed more efficiently. The early greenhouses were made of somewhat opaque and irregular glass and heated mainly by hot air, either from flues in the wall or under the floor, while additional heat was provided by piles of fermenting tan bark. This seems to have resulted in a very dry atmosphere, which suited plants from Australia and S. Africa, but was inimical to plants from the moister tropics. The invention of the circulating boiler and the use of cast-iron pipes as units of heating started early in the century and became further refined as time went on. Since the majority of bedding plants needed a greenhouse for their preservation, the large-scale growing of such plants could not take place until economically possible. Of course the larger nurseries had had stoves and greenhouses for years, but these would have been limited in extent and the purchasers chiefly those sufficiently rich to have greenhouses of their own. Sheet glass, a circulating boiler and the repeal of the tax on glass vastly increased this number.

Another determining factor seems to have been the introduction to commerce of the dwarf scarlet geranium. Scarlet geraniums had been grown for a long time, but they tended to be grown as shrubs. In the *Floricultural Cabinet* for 1841 (p. 16) there is a short article on managing the scarlet geranium and it is assumed that these plants will be grown for some time to come. 'When the plants are two or three years old their stems assume a firm woody habit, and produce abundance of the finest and the largest flowers.' They were often planted out in the summer but if 'planted in the border of a greenhouse, or in a large box, and trained to a trellis . . . it will live many years and attain the height of twenty feet'. Such plants would be covered with flowers from June until November. The coming of 'Tom Thumb' changed that, although, as we have seen, there do seem to have been other compact forms available.

'Tom Thumb' was raised originally in a private garden in Nottinghamshire as a seedling from one of the taller horsehoe scarlets, which had been growing in a vase edged with white ivy-leaved geraniums, so there may possibly have been some hybridisation. This was in 1836. The plant was propagated and circulated privately until some nurseryman saw it and purchased it. It was not available for distribution until 1844, the year which saw the first appearance of General Tom Thumb in London, which accounts for the name and enables us to date its release. The presence of a brilliant flower with a very prolonged flowering season was obviously an impetus in the desire for massing flowers, which had been advocated by Loudon as early as 1826, and which was becoming increasingly popular, although not without some dissent.

In the late 1820s one of the sights of London was the tulips in Groom's famous nursery at Walworth. These were planted in a very higgledy-piggledy manner and in 1827 in the *Gardener's Magazine* he gives a planting plan for a tulip bed in which seventy different tulips are planted; each one being different. This article is followed by a long postscript from Loudon himself, in which he declares his opposition to the 'greatest possible mixture' and complains that gardeners confuse 'mixture' with 'variety'.

'Variety is not produced by mixture, but by a succession of different things. Every part of a mass, formed on the principle of mixture, is the same in appearance, and the general effect monotonous; but every part of a varied whole differs from every other part and the general effect is harmonious.' His recommendation for tulip beds, for example, is 'to place all the Bybloemens in a bed by themselves, and all the bulbs of each variety of Bybloemen together, and again those varieties adjoining each other which are most alike. The only farther requisite in arranging a bed . . . is the choice of a succession of leading colours; that is, supposing all the shades of any one colour disposed of, what colour should be taken next? A practical answer to this question is, recollect the order of colours in the rainbow, and if at any time you are at a loss, ask an artist of any kind, from a milliner girl upwards.'

There were no bedding plants in 1827 in our current sense of the term, but here, already, is its conception. Loudon's excellent advice to plant in masses rather than in single specimens was, indeed, acted upon, but not without some criticism. Here is an pseudonymous writer ('Flora') in the *Floricultural Cabinet* for 1845 (p. 74):

'Much has been said in commendation of the modern fashion of planting the flower clumps of the garden and pleasure ground with but one kind of flower. The effect, in my opinion, is almost always bad; there is as much glare and want of relief in a great bed of Roses, Geraniums, Irises &c., as in the old plan of many species, and with less variety . . . a clump solely of the China, or any other kind of Rose, as is often seen in the midst of a grass plot, seems to me as glaring as would be a nosegay wholly of Roses; and, in the case of Irises &c. there is the further great objection that a week's display in spring is purchased with months of subsequent barrenness and deformity.

'In the new plan of planting flowers, as of shrubs, the professed object is a more close imitation of nature; but it may be doubted whether the object is better attained in one case than the other. It is true that we more frequently see wild flowers growing in masses than singly; but these masses are seldom large, and are almost constantly more or less intermixed with or skirted by other plants.'

Clever 'Flora' seems to have put her (his?) finger on two salient facts. The first that the bedding system entailed long periods when the beds were of little interest is one that is to be repeated by every critic on the subject from Shirley Hibberd to Robinson and his crowd of followers. The appeal to nature is more crucial. That it should ever have been made with regard to the bedding system is rather surprising, but we invariably find gardeners requiring their plants to look natural. Now a garden is highly artificial in every way and few people ever seem to have decided whether by 'natural' they mean that the plants look suitably placed in the garden – which I suspect is what they do intend – or whether they mean that the plants look as though they were native wild flowers, harmoniously arranged.

We find this confusion of thought in almost all writings on the subject and although the ideal English garden is said to be a 'natural' garden, what is generally meant is that it is informal. Of course, once the return to the formal geometric gardens of the Tudors was made, as was about to happen at this point in the nineteenth century, any suggestion that the result could not be artificial would have been ludicrous. Indeed, as the century progressed garden design did sometimes become somewhat ludicrous as, for example, when the Tudor idea of filling the knots with coloured earths during the winter months became popular. Shirley Hibberd, who is the key figure for the mid-century as Loudon was for the earlier part, would have nothing to do with it:

'The working out of a great design in coloured earths and flower beds is the most complicated, and generally speaking, the least satisfactory form of the parterre. It has this advantage, that during the winter it affords "something to look at", but the corresponding disadvantage that nobody wants to see it. A favourite idea with artists in this line of business is to draw out on a gigantic scale, a group of rose, shamrock and thistle in coloured earths and box embroidery, and while the thing is new it looks tolerably well; but the majority of people do not keep themselves under control when tempted to indulge a smile as they admire it. Generally speaking, the design vanishes in summer, that is to say, when the beds are full of flowers, the coloured earths that mark out the design are so completely extinguished that, even with a key plan in one's hand, it would be hard to see where the thistle begins and the shamrock leaves off . . . The principle materials employed for the intersecting walks in these designs are pounded Derbyshire spar (white), pounded brick (red), pounded slate (blue), pounded coal (black), and sifted gravel grit (yellowish grey).'

It is sad to have to state that the Royal Horticultural Society's garden at South Kensington employed these devices.

Let us return, however, to the time when these practices were just starting. In 1845, Louisa Johnstone of Dublin was writing, 'The flower gardens are now, during the summer months, in many cases almost exclusively decorated with exotics; and too much cannot be said in favour of a practice that enables them to rival, for a time, the sun-lit scenes of happier climes, from which we have lately received many plants so exquisitely lovely when displaying their beauty in masses, that without them our gardens would be blank indeed. What, in all the range of floral beauty, unlimited as it is, could compensate us for the loss of even that single group, the Verbenas?'

This feeling was generally accepted, but there soon seems to have come a realisation that the blaze of colour resulting from the bedding system could be too overwhelming. Recourse was made to a publication by a Frenchman, M. Chevreul, who had published a volume entitled *De la loi du contraste simultane des couleurs*, which was translated into English in 1858. It had previously been summarised by Dr. Lindley in the *Gardeners' Chronicle* for December 1849, and was regarded as a guide by the more artistic of those laying out beds. M. Chevreul indeed gave a few examples of gardening practice to be followed. It is difficult to give a precis and a waste of space to give more, but an extract will give the flavour of his argument.

'It is always satisfactory to combine complementary colours, such as Red and Green, Orange and Blue, Greenish yellow and violet, and dark blue with orange yellow. If two colours that are close to each other are put in juxtaposition, each will modify the other. For example if you place Red and Orange next to each other, the red appears tinged with violet while the orange tends towards yellow. Colours are also heightened by being contrasted with white, while combinations with grey are usually satisfactory. However when complementary colours are placed together they are not usually improved by the addition of white, but with non-complementary colours the addition of white may

improve matters. For example Red and Violet are a bad combination, this can be improved by white, red, violet, white, but
best of all is white red, white violet; in fact keep clashing colours
away from each other.'
When the work was published in English the editor of the *Floral
World* (I am not sure if Hibberd was already editing it at that
date) wrote:

'If you look round the gardens just now, you will see many
examples of geraniums and calceolarias in juxtaposition . . . but
the effect is a vulgar glare of colour which tires the eye and
gives no pleasure to a cultivated taste.' So much for the theory
that all Victorian bedding was of this glaring nature. In point
of fact, the range of bedding plants, even in the early days, was
very large. Here is a list, with all cultivar names omitted from
the *Floricultural Cabinet* for June 1850. Geraniums (which
included rose, pink, crimson, salmon, cherry and other varying
colours) 18cvs. Hybrids of scented-leaved with Regal Pelargoniums. These were known as Fancy pelargoniums and 6 cvs
were recommended, ranging in colour from red to purple.
Bouvardias, apparently including a yellow-flowered plant;
alstromerias – I cannot think which species could be adapted to
pot culture during the winter and could then be planted out in
the summer, but there was a large choice of species available in
1850, many more than nowadays – *Cuphea ignea* and *C.
strigulosa*; *Anagallis linifolia* cvs – there were a large number of
these in blue and various shades of red. Lobelias, both the dwarf
blues and the tall scarlets, appeared in the list, and alonsoas, of
which two species were apparently available of which *A. acuti-
folia* was taller than *A. incisa*. Among the heliotropes the
'Voltaireanum' had deep blue flowers, but was rather a shy
grower, while 'Triomphe de Leigh' had huge heads of white
flowers. *Anemone japonica* was still, apparently, treated as half
hardy. There were a large number of pentstemons. In 1850 there
were a number of calceolarias, at which we will look more closely
in a minute. *Mesembryanthemum tricolor* and other *Mesembryanthemum* species are perhaps unexpected here. There were
a very large number of petunias, which seem then to have been
very vigorous plants requiring to be pegged down. *Oxalis
bowieii* and *O. lutea* (is this *pes-caprae*?) and *Silene schafta* are

all somewhat unexpected. *Dianthus chinensis* and *Phlox drummondii* were also recommended, which are still used today.

There is something of a mystery attached to the calceolarias of those early days. In the *Floricultural Cabinet* for 1854 a Mr. John Burley lists 24 cvs as among the best bedding Calceolarias and they were obviously in a considerable colour range. 'Masterpiece' was a 'fine dark crimson'; 'Superba' was 'orange and crimson'; 'Amazon' was crimson-maroon and 'Magnificent' was 'rich crimson with a yellow cap'. There were numerous other crimsons, as well as the expected yellows, orange, bronze and brown. These were all recommended for bedding. In his *Rustic Adornments* of 1857 Hibberd mentions fewer crimsons and more yellows but adds 'Purity', 'a lively white sort, which beds well in poor sandy soil'. Yet when he published *The Amateur's Flower Garden* in 1871 he recommended only a few yellow-flowering plants, ignores the white and said, 'The red and brown varieties are simply useless'. From his piece about this plant we may get a suggestion for the reason. 'It is not uncommon,' he writes, 'for all the calceolarias in the country to perish about the middle of July, leaving the parterres they should have adorned with masses of golden flowers abominably ugly with their withered stumps.' Hibberd thought that this was due to putting out the plants too late, so that they could not root properly: 'In fact the principal reason of the failure of the calceolaria in a hot dry season is defective roothold, the result of planting late in poor soil, the plants having been already nearly starved to death in pots as a preparation for their final extinction.' This may well be true, but does not explain why the early crimson and mottled hybrids should have suddenly become useless. The brown one, about which he is equally condemnatory was certainly available before 1939 and, for all I know, may be still – and it was quite satisfactory. I have never seen any other reference to the white one.

Among the plants listed by Hibberd in 1857 are abronias. These 'sand verbenas' could never have been very easy to grow and were probably disappointing in wet or cold summers. So their disappearance, although regrettable, is not surprising, and as the craze persisted the number of flowering plants was drastically reduced.

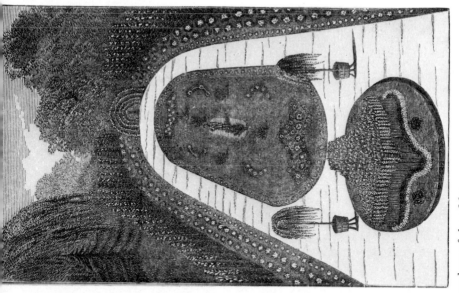

14, 15 Two small suburban gardens of the 1860s

16 Longford Castle. The Victorian architectural garden; more or less a return to the Tudors and like them designed to be seen from above rather than at eye level, but differing in its brilliant colouring owing to Victorian bedding where the Tudors had to have coloured earths

Writing in 1864 in the *Floral World* (p. 196) Hibberd says: 'As for the odds and ends of the bedding list that, previous to the year 1860, made so many features of interest, they are nearly all swept away. Leptodactylon (= Gilia) californicum, Agathaea coelestis, Bouvardias, Anagallis, Heliotropes, Mimulus, Senecios and many other truly beautiful subjects . . . have passed into comparative obscurity.' This was due, in large part, to the great strides that were being made in the breeding of the Zonal pelargoniums, which were now available in a number of colours, but which had also been developed to give a number of cvs with coloured leaves.

Various blue lobelias were also being employed, but perhaps the main development from the early days was the increasing use of ornamental foliage. Silvers ranged from the dwarf *Cerastium tomentosa* and *C. biebersteinii* (said to be preferable) to *Gnaphalium lanatum* and *Antennaria dioica* for edgings, while *Centaurea ragusina* and *C. candidissima* were taller subjects. Darker notes were provided by *Coleus, Perilla nankinensis*, various *Amaranthus* species, and even exceptionally dark purple-leaved beet and *Atriplex*. This was also the time when variegated foliage was being used more and more. Many plants with variegated leaves were brought back from Japan by Robert Fortune in 1860 and even more had been assiduously cultivated by John Salter at Hammersmith, who was responsible for a plant which he called *Ajuga reptans* 'Purpurascens', which was said to be 'for all practical purposes . . . nearest to black of any bedding plant known'. This almost black-leaved plant seems to have been lost. As the number of coloured-leaved plants available increased they were used more and more extensively. As writers of the time pointed out, cold and wet summers would prevent the plants from flowering freely, while the coloured foliage was always present. Moreover, some effect was present as soon as the beds were planted up, whereas one had to wait for the blooms of the flowering bedders.

The final phase came with the introduction of very dwarf, coloured-leaved plants such as alternantheras and iresines. These, if planted close together, could be made into intricate patterns and the result was known as carpet bedding. This was really the dream of the Tudor gardeners and, as might have been expected, was hotly decried by mediaevalists such as William Morris and all who professed to love the good old days. However, this reversal to mediaeval taste was only possible for those with ample staff and greenhouse space and thus only existed in public parks and in a few gardens of the *nouveau riche*. It is still occasionally practised in public parks and now has a certain period charm, but it is certainly the ultimate negation of 'natural' gardening. Some of these foliage introductions were unfortunate. In the late 1850s Van Houtte introduced the bronze-leaved form of *Oxalis corniculata* and it seems incredible to think that people once paid good money to obtain this pestilential weed.

As might be expected, the main displays of bedding were in public parks and among these Battersea Park was outstanding for what was termed subtropical gardening, a system originated by M. Barillet in Paris. Here, the emphasis was entirely on foliage, but generally on plants from the greenhouse, which resulted not only in the planting out of such subjects as Tree ferns, bananas, *Ficus* etc. during the summer, but in the introduction to cultivation of a large number of large-leaved plants. In 1869, Messrs. Rollisson issued a seed list for suitable subjects, which included a number of *Cleome* species; several Daturas; numerous forms of *Nicotiana* and *Ricinus*; a huge number of *Solanum* species; a large number of *Canna* hybrids; *Schefflera venulosa* and wigandias. Most of these have dropped out of cultivation, but some may make a comeback as house plants. The subtropical garden also increased the spread of another pestilential plant, *Polygonum cuspidatum* the Japanese bamboo, which as a novelty in the late 1860s made an impressive sight growing on its own in Battersea Park; its ineradicability only became manifest later.

The superintendent of Battersea was an interesting figure, John Gibson. He had worked at Chatsworth under Paxton and had been sent to India in 1836, mainly to collect a plant of *Amerstia nobilis*. But while there he had collected many plants, most notably dendrobiums and *Aeschynanthus* from the Khasia Hills, and was responsible for many first introductions. The primary aim of the subtropical garden seems to have been the production of very large leaves, but soon various coloured leaves, mainly of *Caladium* and *Cordyline* species and later *Begonia*

Rex hybrids, laid the foundations of the modern enthusiasm for coloured-leaved houseplants. The habit seems to have started in 1864, but it was the later 1860s and early 70s which saw the real glory of Battersea.

Although very suitable for public displays, such as the Crystal Palace, the RHS Gardens at Kensington and various public parks, the bedding system was not really suitable for small gardens. Perhaps one of the most telling explanations of this attitude came in the *Floral World* for April 1864. This comment is again by Hibberd and he starts off by saying that 'in this its seventh year it has to pronounce for the seventh time that gardens are not made for bedders, though bedders are undoubtedly made for gardens'. What he objected to was 'that in thousands of private gardens they (e.g. bedding plants) absorbed all the gardener's time, all the master's money . . . and in return for this wholesale and general absorption, gave a display of colour during only four or five months of the year, and that very often the same every succeeding year . . . The consequence of the usurpation by the bedders has been the deterioration of horticulture, in some respects, among the class to whom it offers the greatest hope of pleasure . . . namely the amateurs who generally only keep one gardener or who perform all the light and amusing operations in their gardens with their own hands. Prohibit these from using bedding plants, and forthwith they will begin to restore to the neglected borders the noble clumps of fragrant white lilies, the patches of Christmas rose, winter aconite, double daisy, polyanthus, primula, Solomon's seal, Indian pink, potentilla, and the thousand other interesting subjects which make no blaze at any season, but are constantly presenting beautiful forms and cheerful colours'. This was a complaint that was to be made with increasing stridency throughout the years. In 1871, William Robinson, Hibberd's protégé, started *The Garden* to combat the bedding system (although he seems to have kept a liking for Gibson's work at Battersea) and in 1883, when the battle was practically won, he produced *The English Flower Garden* to praise the use of hardy herbaceous subjects and to denigrate what he referred to as tropical weeds. He was late in the field, but he had a gift for vituperation, which seems to have made people pay more heed to him than they had to earlier writers. However the battle has never been won. The bedding system is as popular today as it was in the 1860s, only in place of geraniums and foliage plants we have H.T. and Floribunda roses. These have the advantage of being hardy, but the objection that the beds are of no interest between October and June is just as valid today as it was in Hibberd's time. Indeed when writing *The Amateur's Flower Garden* he said, 'The question will occur where a [rose] garden should be formed, within view of the windows or far away. We reply, "far away"; for a rose garden should be in its season a wonder to be sought, as, when its season is past, it is a wilderness to be avoided.'

In the same book, Hibberd goes some way to making the bedding system more acceptable. He starts off by saying that 'the bedding system as commonly understood is an idea only half developed', and goes on to point out that it is only brilliant for three months and 'for the remaining nine months of the year it is a dreary blank . . . Yet,' he says, 'for the sake of this temporary glory, ten thousand gardens, that would otherwise have been rich in gardens of a permanent character, and comparatively exhaustless in interest, have been reduced to the condition of manufactories, and the summer show, as a proof to all observers of what the factory could produce, has been considered sufficient return . . .' This factory analogy is interesting, for many observers have felt that the wheel-like beds and the flaming colours of the bedding system did reflect the industrial revolution; the concept is somewhat doubtful, but there certainly is an analogy between them.

Hibberd's suggested amplification of the bedding system amounts, to all intents and purposes, to the methods of the present day, although his suggestions are somewhat more elaborate than most practitioners will accept. He suggested that for the spring the beds should be planted with bulbs and other spring flowers, among which he lists forget-me-nots, iberis, alyssum, pansies, daisies and polyanthus. As soon as these were over they were removed and the summer bedders inserted, but towards the end of September these too were removed and replaced by 'early-flowering pompone chrysanthemums', which might be expected to prolong the display until mid-November, when the chrysanthemums would be removed and the spring bedders inserted. Nowadays, the insertion of late-flowering plants is usually omitted and formal bedding has a spring display and a summer display.

The introduction of the bedding system led to some changes in bulb breeding. When it was first suggested, tulips were still mainly grown as florists' flowers, with the emphasis on flaming and pencilling. The call for regular bedding tulips resulted in the emergence of the Darwin strain with plain colours. Similarly, very little work had been done on breeding daffodils, although this was started in the 1860s, and here again, the call for bedding plants gave an impetus to the breeder. The one bulb that was generally available was the hyacinth. Tulips, known as 'Breeders' could be purchased according to colour, but they were never named, might come to uneven heights, which would be unsatisfactory in a bed. They were originally bought by florists who would hope that they would eventually 'break'. We now know that this 'breaking', in which the petals are striped and flared, is due to a virus infection, but formerly there were many very peculiar recipes as to how to make your tulip break.

One group of summer bedding plant has been omitted from our lists, which seems to have been extensively used and which, one feels, must have been somewhat different from the plants of the same name today. These were the dwarf, or 'Tom Thumb', nasturtiums, which were available in a variety of colours, mainly pale yellow and orange-brown, but there were also scarlets and bright yellows.

Although one can sympathise with the bedding system, and even though one may disapprove of it, one can have little except horror for most of the ornaments that found their way in the mid-nineteenth-century garden. Summer houses ranged from replicas of Swiss chalets to so-called rustic works, made of untrimmed logs, and these would also be used for chairs and tables. Sometimes, the rustic tables looked as though they were made of wood, but turned out to be made of painted pottery or wrought iron, or even Ransome's artificial stone. Beds would be surrounded with wire, so that they resembled enormous baskets. Shirley Hibberd in his *Rustic Adornments* wrote, in 1857: 'As to summer houses and arbours generally, there never was so much ugliness scattered about the world as of late years has been sprinkled over suburban gardens.' But, he then goes on to say: 'Summer houses in the Chinese style have a fantastic and pleasing effect if well placed.' By 'well placed' he means that the 'approach . . . should be by a clean winding walk, with a well-cut box edging and a bright display of the finest flowers and ever-greens . . . The construction itself cannot be too elaborately decorated; quaint carving, geometrical ornaments and filigree work, the whole gaily painted and kept fresh, all give it an appropriate character.' On the other hand: 'The genuine rustic arbour must be of a totally different character. It must be in the midst of shrubby and rustic scenery, on a mound well sprinkled with ferns, with perhaps a rill of water below, and a mossy walk leading from it to dark wilderness scenery.'

Besides these buildings there were rustic tables and chairs, which were later to be replaced by cast-iron garden furniture, which looks rather elegant nowadays, when painted white, but which in those days was usually painted green and was much less attractive. Besides this, the garden might be ornamented by statuary and by large terracotta urns and ornamental pots, which would be planted up with suitable plants such as fuchsias during the summer. In the centre of the formal garden there could be either a sun dial or an ornamental water with a fountain. These fountains ranged from the rustic, which was only an artificial cascade, to elaborate designs. We learn that Messrs. Cottam and Hallen 'have given a large share of their attention to the pro-ductions of fountains in iron and artificial stone, and the result is all that could be desired for the gratification of artistic taste'. Moreover iron was 'not only capable of assuming graceful out-lines' but tended to be more durable than stone, as well as being cheaper. Artificial stone was also much used for edgings to beds and borders and consisted of a triangular tile which had a moulded edge. This was sunk in the ground with only the moulded scroll visible. These do appear to have been quite indestructible and can still be found in many parks and gardens. They were of an innocuous slate colour.

The period is also noteworthy for the introduction of lawn mowers, so that it was no longer necessary to scythe the lawns.

Hand-pushed mowing machines were invented some time in the 1830s and were popular by the '60s, while larger expanses were catered for by horse-drawn machines.

—— 8 ——

The Nineteenth Century:
Part 3

So far, we have been speaking of the general mixed flower garden, but the nineteenth century also saw the construction of numbers of specialist gardens. Of these the most recondite was the mossery. Even so, there was one nurseryman, a Mr. Stark of Edinburgh,[1] who offered mosses in his catalogue. The subject was treated in the *Floral World* for 1869. The pseudonymous author starts by saying that the study and culture of mosses is never likely to be as popular as that of ferns, but, on the other hand, the fact that they look at their best from November to February, when the garden is generally dull, should, he says, tell in their favour. Moreover, they will thrive where few other plants do:

'I think that few subjects would . . . be more suitable for growing where the only space . . . consists of a small back-yard, overshadowed by other houses. A really fine collection may be grown in a space ten feet square.

'The moss garden formed by Mr. Summers, in the garden of Mr. Mongredien at Forest Hill, is about the best that has yet come under public notice . . . The rockery, upon which the mosses were grown, was constructed with burrs arranged in terraces and supplied with water at the summit, so as to cause a trickling down from terrace to terrace, until at the base the various rivulets formed a pool. The mosses were planted on the ledges and amongst the burrs, those requiring a special soil having their wants provided for; and thus some hundreds of species were brought under the eye at once.'

The writer points out that stone was preferable to burrs, but might be too expensive. He also gives some details about collecting and establishing the plants. This idea gets taken up from time to time, but although mosses grow readily where not wanted, as in lawns, they are not easily established in cultivation.

One would like to know more about Mr. Mongredien and Mr. Summers, who seem to have been both skilful cultivators and original gardeners. They it was who were responsible for the concept of the *Spergula* lawn, which had a brief renown in the late 1850s and early '60s. In this, grass was replaced by *Spergula* (=*Sagina*) *caespitosa* which, when well managed, apparently looked better than grass, but only very few people ever managed it successfully and it soon sank into oblivion.

The moss garden may have been rather a rarefied idea, but the fernery was very popular and long remained so. Hibberd gave the fernery a whole chapter in his *Rustic Adornments* and it is understandable that, after the glare of geraniums and other bedding plants, the soft greens and delicate shapes of fern fronds would provide a delicious contrast. Rather oddly, they were very often grown against rocks, and it seems probable that most of the early rock gardens, to which we will come next, were mainly planted with ferns.

Although natural ferns were admired, more admiration was given to unusual varieties, in which the pinnules might be increased or where they might be much shorter than normal. Thus there were numerous varieties of each fern, so that the statement in Hibberd's book that Mr. Robert Sim, of Foot's Cray, had catalogued 440 ferns is less surprising than appears at first, as there might well be twenty forms of the male fern or of the lady fern, of which fifteen varieties were named by John Smith in 1866 in his *Ferns, British and Foreign*. As many as fifty-five of the Hart's tongue were listed, which sounds as though a lot of very minute differences had been named. In the preface to his second edition in 1876 Mr. Smith says that Mr. Stansfield's catalogue contains nearly 500 names: 'These consist of abnormal forms of a few British species, principally of Asplenium filix-foemina, Lastrea filix-mas, Polystichum aculeatum, Scolopendrium vulgare, Lomaria spicant and Polypodium vulgare, to which numbers of new forms are yearly being added by cultivation, or found wild.'

Hibberd was presumably only echoing established taste when he wrote that 'ferns never show to such good effect as when their emerald feathery fronds droop over masses of dark stones'. Moreover – 'It is impossible for any one to give much attention to ferns without attaining to very correct and chaste notions of taste: and we might say that the love of ferns is always an accompaniment of correct ideas of embellishment.' Many growers did plant their ferns in the most romantic situations, with crags and old roots of trees and a variety of other devices, which scarcely suggest the currently correct ideas of embellishment. None the less, it may be that modern gardeners are wrong, and that this extension of Gothic romance into the garden may have had its charms. In contemporary illustrations they look thrilling, but since almost all depictions of gardens, whether by drawing or by photography seem deceptive, perhaps too much attention should not be paid to that. The scale and perspective always seem excessive, so that a small plot looks like an acre in extent and fronds, that may be 18 ins. long look as though they were at least twice that.

The interest in monstrous forms seems to have lasted for about thirty years, from 1840 to 1870, although normal ferns were popular in gardens both long before and after that date. It was not until after 1918 that they started to lose their association with shady parts of the garden. Since then they have become the plants of very few, but, with the renewed interest in attractive foliage, they are now starting to make a comeback.

Besides the interest in hardy ferns, there was an almost greater interest in exotic ferns, which needed greenhouse conditions. This trend can probably be dated as starting after 1860 when the attractive maidenhair ferns, collected by Veitch's collector Richard Pearce in Chile and Peru, were released to commerce. The interest increased throughout the century as more and more people could afford greenhouses and conservatories. Ferns were also used for floral decorations. One always thinks of trails of *Smilax* and *Asparagus plumosus* trailing over the Victorian dining table, but these seem, rather, to have been Edwardian and the professional writers on flower arranging always recommended the climbing fern, *Lygodium scandens.*

The fernery has had a rather short existence but the rock garden has persisted for far longer. Here, however, we must make a distinction between rocks placed for their own sakes – a curious, apparently unmotivated parallel with Japanese gardens – and that curious assembly that was called a rockery. Rockwork had existed for a long time. In his book on gardens Sir William Temple states that the 'most perfect figure of a garden I ever saw, either at home or abroad, was that of Moor Park in Hertfordshire, when I knew it about 30 years ago', that is, around 1660. Among the various parts of the garden was one that was 'very wild, shady, and adorned with rough rock-work and fountains'. Indeed, all the grottoes and hermitages that adorned gardens in baroque times later contained rock-work of a sort, but this was generally composed of rough blocks cemented together and contained no deliberately planted vegetation, although it was always possible that ferns might establish themselves.

In the latter part of the eighteenth century Forsyth, Miller's successor, made a so-called rock garden at the Physic Garden at Chelsea. This was principally composed of geological specimens brought back from Iceland by Sir Joseph Banks, and we do not know how, or indeed if it was planted, but it seems probable that it was occupied mainly by ferns and the easier saxatile plants, such as stonecrops and house leeks. At Fonthill, Beckford had an alpine garden and grotto, but even less is known of this.

Thanks to an advertisement in volume 6 of Loudon's *Gardener's Magazine* for 1830 we know something more of a rather extraordinary erection belonging to a Mr. Brookes – so extraordinary, indeed, that it seems worth reproducing almost the whole of the piece.

'Mr. Brookes, being about to change his residence, begs to acquaint Mr. Loudon, that he has for sale an extensive and picturesque mass of rock-work, composed chiefly of considerable pieces of the rock of Gibraltar, adapted to the purpose of a vivarium, at present occupied by an eagle, and several smaller rapacious birds. The structure is excavated in different parts for the seclusion of its tenants. The four principal entrances of the adyta are ample and arched with rude portions of rock: there

are likewise numerous cryptae arranged irregularly for various
animals, and subterranean passages intersecting each other for
their convenience and retirement. The whole covers an area of
about 30 ft., and is upwards of 10 ft. in height, somewhat in the
shape of a truncated cone, on the surface of which there is a
spacious reservoir for fishes, aquatic plants, and oceanic birds,
with a jet d'eau in the centre, ascending through an interesting
specimen of rock, much elevated above the level of the water,
which is prevented from overflowing by a siphon, which conveys
it through the mouth of an antique head of a gigantic reptile,
nearly resembling that of an Icthyosaurus. The interstices of the
rock are verdant with alpine and appropriate indigenous plants;
these, descending over the stones, embellish and augment the
pleasing appearance of the fabric, which would prove a beautiful
object in an arboretum, or at the termination of a vista . . .
Occupying an angle in the garden there is a pilgrim's cell, constructed in a great measure of the jaws of a whale, having
furniture manufactured of the bones of the same animal, and
lighted by a circular stained glass window.'
One wonders on what the alpine and indigenous plants were
living, and how anyone could manage to transport so bulky a
piece.

During the 1830s, at Hoole House, near Chester, Lady
Broughton constructed a very extraordinary rock garden, which
was described by Loudon, both in the *Gardener's Magazine* for
1838 and in his *Villa Garden*. Basically, the garden consisted of a
large lawn containing a number of circular flower beds (designed
as baskets) surrounded on three sides by rock-work:

'The design of the rock-work was taken from a small model representing the mountains of Savoy with the valley of Chamouni.
It has been the work of many years to complete it, the difficulty
being to make it stand against the weather. Rain washed away
the soil and frost melted the stones; several times the main wall
failed from the weight put upon it. The walls and the foundation
are built of the red sandstone of the county; and the other
materials have been collected from various quarters, chiefly
from Wales; but it is now so generally covered with creeping
and alpine plants that it all mingles together in one mass. The
outline, however, is carefully preserved; and the part of the

model that represents "La mer de glace" is worked with grey limestone, quartz and spar. It has no cells for plants: the spaces are filled up with broken fragments of white marble, to look like snow: and the spar is intended for the glacier . . .

'The rock-work is planted with a selection of the most care and beautiful alpines . . . each placed in a nidus of suitable soil, and the surface protected from the weather by broken fragments of stone, clean-washed river gravel, the debris of decaying rock, moss, or other suitable substances, according as the object was to retain moisture; to evaporate moisture in order to prevent the plants from damping off; to increase the heat, in which case dark fragments of stone are used; or to diminish it, which is effected by the employment of white pebbles, which, by reflecting the light and heat, keep the ground cool.'

The whole fantastic erection seems to have shown a sophistication in growing alpines which was far in advance of its time. Loudon lists the plants employed, which included all the alpines then available, among them such unusual subjects as *Calceolaria fothergillii*, *Jeffersonia diphylla*, claytonias, *Coptis trifolia*, pinguiculas, pyrolas, *Mitella* and *Tiarella cordifolia*. Robinson saw the garden in 1868, when it was still in good order and to which beehives shaped like Swiss chalets had been added.

Rock-work on a different scale was used by William Wells in his garden at Redleaf, at Penshurst, which was described by Loudon in his *Gardener's Magazine* for 1839. This seems to have been altogether a rather curious place, with an English garden and a Dutch garden, in which were placed a rustic billiard room, and which seems to have included a Chinese dairy, although 'the dairy is not used as such, but is merely to be considered as a collection of Chinese dairy porcelain'. There was also an experimental garden reserved for the plant breeding activities of the gardener Joseph Wells, who is said to have raised the first dwarf dahlias in 1825. But the most unusual feature was the rocky lawn, which ended with a precipice. When Mr. Wells took over Redleaf he observed some projecting rocks, as well as the remains of an old quarry, so that rock was easy to come by. Apparently, the rocks were used for enclosing raised beds and as protection for tender plants: 'The plants in the rocky beds are partly half-hardy; such as fuchsia, myrtles, and other plants usually planted against conservative walls; magnolias; a fine collection of azaleas and rhododendrons, particularly on the rocky precipice; Berberis, Mahonia, Garrya, and, in short, all the finer shrubs that are rather tender and some of the more rare trees.'

The connection between rocks and alpine plants seems to have come about rather slowly. Writing in 1849 in the *Floricultural Cabinet* (p. 106) 'An Amateur' says that they have long been favourites of his and 'it has afforded me great pleasure to observe that the last two seasons nearly all the principal horticultural and floricultural societies have admitted them . . . At the Chiswick, Regent's Park and Surrey Gardens shows, very extensive collections were exhibited'. The writer notes that 'in England, alpine plants are often planted out on rock-work and in shady borders; but experience shows that they never succeed long or well in such situations'. He therefore suggests growing them in pots and overwintering them in a cold frame. The soil is to be half light, sandy loam and half good peat, but if the loam is not sandy a sixth part of silver sand should be added 'and a little well decomposed leaf-mould will be a beneficial addition . . . The summer station for alpines should be chosen with an aspect as near north as possible, and where they will not be exposed to the sun more than two hours in the morning; but they must by no means be under the shade and drip of trees. They should be placed on, or plunged in, finely-sifted coal ashes, and every means taken to keep worms from them . . . too much attention cannot be paid to watering them, in order to keep them and the ground around them constantly moist; but they should never be indiscriminately watered.'

This insistence on a cool, shady situation is rather odd, as many of the genera he recommends, such as *Aubrieta* and *Dianthus* are usually thought of as sun lovers. He lists sixty-nine genera as containing the most showy species, but suggests that there were many more he could have mentioned. The list contains few surprises, but does contain a large number of the best alpine genera.

In his *Floral World* article of 1866, William Robinson says, 'The rarest thing in British Gardens is a good rock-work, and when one is met with that which is satisfactory from an artistic point of view, it is usually covered with rank vegetation sufficient to destroy all the chances the real alpines might have if planted. Probably the noblest rock-works in England are those at Chatsworth, where the noble wood-crowned hill behind the "palace of the Peak" suits the formation of such, and there they have been certainly made on a grand scale and by a tasteful hand. Ferns and herbaceous plants etc. predominate, but the dwarf and genuine alpine plant is not favoured: indeed the great shoals and clefts do not suit things which like the full sun and free air, however much they may relish abundant water at the root.'

Robinson was writing at a time when the rockery was starting to turn into the alpine garden. According to Henri Correvon, the first alpine garden was made by Boissier, the great Swiss botanist, at Geneva. But as far as England is concerned, we can probably date the alpine garden – as distinct from rock-work or a rockery – from 1859 when Messrs. Backhouse of York, one of the greatest nursery firms of the day, constructed their very large and famous rock garden. In the article already cited, Robinson says 'it has been the result of an expenditure which no other nurseryman would risk, and a result of knowledge of the natural habits of alpine vegetation on the part of one of the firm, which few other botanists possess'. Nearly 500 tons of sandstone were employed in this splendid construction, which was so arranged that 'every sort of aspect or nook that could be desired for a plant is at hand, and thus plants the most diverse in character are accommodated happily within a few feet of each other: under the shade of the great stones by the water, New Zealand filmy ferns; a few feet higher up natives of Arctic Europe; and on the top, in the full sun and free air, the choicest gems of temperate parts of Europe and America'.

The interest aroused by this was such that, in 1865, the firm issued a catalogue entirely comprised of alpine plants. I have not been able to find a copy of this, but have found, in the RHS Lindley Library, the alpine catalogue of 1867 and it is worth devoting some attention to this. There is a very interesting preface, which contains, *in parvo*, so much good sense about the cultivation of alpine plants that it is worth giving some extracts.

'With something less than 25s. worth of rocks (costing here 9s. per ton) we have formed a rocky bank upon which many scores of choice Alpines thrive admirably. For, though contact with the rock is necessary for some, it is not needful for all. The improved drainage afford by a bank 3 or 4 feet high (in the composition of which a large proportion of rough sand should generally be used) quite suffices for the wants of many species; as, though "true mountaineers" they inhabit the glades and plateaus of alpine regions, where there is often a large area of rich vegetable soil without rock.

'One thing must constantly be borne in mind, that it is *an error* to suppose that "little plants" require but very shallow soil! As narrow a crack or crevice as you please, only it must lead to an abundant supply for deeply rooting, hungry fibres, that hate both "Starvation" and the irregularity of temperature and moisture inseparable from a shallow soil. Gentiana verna is a *little* plant, its tuft of leaves rarely attaining the elevation of an inch; but we are not exceeding the truth in saying that it both likes (and apparently requires for full development) *eighteen inches depth at least* of rich fibrous loam, interspersed thickly with blocks of limestone; it is almost impossible to get "into the bottom" of its far-rooting tiny threads in a native locality . . .

'There are many alpine plants which are found chiefly (and perhaps some exclusively) in the grit of decomposed rocks carried down by torrents etc. In this there is sometimes very little admixture of earth, though what little there is, is usually of the richest kind. Crushed millstone grit or coarse sandstone forms an excellent substitute and should, if possible, be largely mingled with the soil of a "rockwork". For some alpines we use equal parts of grit and earth – a mixture of rich loam and peat or leaf-mould. If not procurable, river sand is the best substitute. Some species grow well in almost pure grit. There are, however, not a few, we have recently ascertained, which though found in grit in a wild state, thrive better in cultivation, if placed in pure loam in a narrow fissure of rock. The simple reason seems to be that they are frozen dry and *kept* dry for months in their own land in winter; while, when planted on rockwork they are necessarily exposed to constant moisure during the winter months with us . . .

'Another most important subject is to *suspend the abundant supply* of moisture essential for health in spring and summer (in imitation of the melting of alpine snows) when the annual growth

17 The bedding system getting fantastic

18 The revolt against glaring colours – subtropical foliage plants
19 The fern garden

is made, so as to coax the plant "to be quiet" as far as possible and prevent a second and enfeebling growth. This seems very important to the alpine Gentians and to the rare Eritrichium nanum. Natural rains will, as a rule, suffice after the end of August and earlier, if the weather be rainy. All artificial irrigation except for bog plants should then cease.'

With such clear and excellent rules, it is not surprising that the interest in alpines increased. Moreover Messrs. Backhouse offered a very large selection of them. Among the novelties of 1867 were *Crocus speciosus; Epigaea repens; Pyxidanthera barbulata; Viola pedata; Drosera filiformis; Pinguicula longifolia; Xerophyllum asphodeloides;Moneses uniflora; Gentiana ciliata* and *G. alpina*. The general list included *Acantholimon glumaceum*; 3 *Cassiope* species; 13 Androsace species (including *A.A. cylindrica, glacialis and helvetica*); *Anemone baldensis* and *A. nuttalliana*; 10 *Arenaria* species; 7 *Astragalus* species; *Callixene polyphylla* (=*Luzuriaga erecta*, a Chilean plant of rather dubious hardiness); 23 *Campanula* species; 13 *Crocus* species, including *C.C. boryi, laevigatus* and *sieberi; Polygonatum roseum*; 18 *Dianthus* species and 5 *Cyclamen*. *Eritrichium nanum* was priced from 7s. 6d. to 10s. 6d. per plant. There were 26 *Gentiana* species, including unusual species such as *GG. crinita, fortunei, gelida* and *utriculosa*. There were 15 *Lilium* species, among which *Fritillaria camschatica* figured; *Meconopsis nepalensis; Myositidium; Mitella pentandra*; a number of *Paeonia* species which are very difficult to identify; 3 species of *Parnassia* and the N. American *Polygala paucifolia*. There were no less than 38 primulas and it is interesting to note that *P. sikkimensis* was still rare and priced at 10s. 6d. a plant, while the N. American *P. parryi* was only 5s. They listed 6 *Pyrola* species, which included plants that are now in other genera; 13 *Ranuculus* species, which included *Callianthemum; Rigidella immaculata*, which is rarely seen nowadays; no less than 69 species of *Saxifraga* including such species as *S.S. aretioldes, androsacea, biflora, juniperina* and *pectinata;* 32 *Sedum* species; 6 *Sisyrinchium* species; 5 *Soldanella* species; 5 *Romulea* species; 5 *Tulipa* species; 18 *Viola* species and 35 orchids.

It is interesting to compare this list with one published twelve years later, when the novelties were *Meconopsis aculeata, Daphne rupestris* and *Sedum sempervivoides*. There were 5 *Calochortus* species. The number of *Campanula* species had increased from 26 to 39, but there were only 8 *Crocus* species which now included *C. imperati* and *C. minimus*. The number of *Dianthus* species had risen from 18 to 26, but the number of *Gentian* species had fallen to 20. In 1867, there were only 2 *Geranium* species listed, but by 1879 this had increased to 13. Previously, there were very few *Iris* species, but now there were no less than 25. *Lewisia rediviva* suddenly appears in the list and the number of lilies went up to 25. There were 6 species of *Linum*, including *L. viscosum*, which always seems reluctant to thrive in Britain. Three hardy *Opuntia* species make a surprising appearance. *Phyteuma comosum* was priced at from 5s. to 7s. 6d. and a surprising novelty (and one to be discouraged) was *Pinguicula vallisneriaefolia*. The number of primulas had increased to 50, saxifragas to 84 and sedums to 51. There were 2 extra *Sisyrinchium* species and 2 less *Romulea* species, only 9 *Viola* species but 10 more hardy orchids.

It was obvious that alpine plants were not only being admired but also assiduously cultivated. In 1870 William Robinson produced his book on the *Alpine Garden*, which he dedicated to Backhouse and which must be regarded as one of his better contributions, and in 1872 and 1874 Wooster produced his *Illustrations of Alpine Plants*. Both he and Hibberd advocated the use of raised beds, where it was not possible to construct a rockery. Here is a description of one such garden at Hornsey, now in north London, but in 1868 a country suburb. It was made by a Mr. Farmer and described by Robinson in the *Floral World*.

'A little bed was dug out in the clay soil to the depth of two feet, and a drain run from it to an outlet near at hand; the bed was filled with fine sandy peat and a little loam and leaf mould, and when nearly full, rustic stones of very different sizes were placed around the margin, so as to raise the bed on an average one foot or so above the turf. More soil was then put in, and a few rough slabs, arranged so as to crop out from the soil in the centre, completed the preparation for the neater Sedums and Sempervivums, such Saxifragas as caesia and rocheliana, such Dianthus as alpinus and petraeus, Mountain Forget-me-nots, Gentians, little spring bulbs, Hepatica angulosa etc.'

This was apparently a great success; the only failure being *Gentiana bavarica*, although *G. verna* thrived. Admittedly, the most brilliant plant was *Calandrinia umbellata*, which is not usually regarded as a good alpine, but Robinson also lists such plants as *Dianthus alpinus, Campanula pulla, Mertensia maritima, Alyssum spinosum, Sedum brevifolium, Androsace lanuginosa* and *Diotis candidissima* – so it was obviously successful. Hibberd suggested that the beds could be raised as high as 4 ft., although no one seems to have suggested the use of dry walling, which is employed nowadays.

Indeed, the 'rocks' of the early rock gardens were their greatest drawback. Messrs. Backhouse may have been able to get rock at 9s. per ton in York, but in the metropolis large rocks were expensive to procure, and the usual base of the rockery was composed of fused bricks from the bottom of brick kilns, which were covered with a sort of clinker and referred to as burrs. These were cheap and easily obtainable, but they were rather unsightly. In unpolluted atmosphere they might soon get covered with lichen and moss, but in smoky London they looked unnatural. Even in my youth there was a rock border in Waterlow Park, Highgate, in which all the 'rocks' were burrs and very unsightly they looked. Such disadvantages did not apply in places near a source of supply and, as rock gardening became increasingly popular and was taken up by moneyed proprietors, rocks were imported to places far from where they normally occurred. Rocks from Westmorland and Bath Stone became increasingly popular as media. Although these large expensive rock gardens belong mainly to the early years of the present century, it may be argued that the whole process continued to develop from the example of Backhouse. We must look at these rock gardens a little more closely in a moment, but first I would like to make a point about dates.

It has always been assumed, chiefly, it must be admitted, on the very shaky authority of Robinson, that during the mid-nineteenth century, every aspect of gardening was sacrificed to the bedding system. This attitude is, to a certain extent, reinforced by the quotation from Hibberd about the herbaceous plants being thrown out to make way for the bedding plants. There must have been some truth in these remarks, although a study of gardening magazines from 1845 onwards does not show any very great emphasis on bedding, rather criticism of its crudity – though with notable exceptions. And, as we have seen, this was also the period which encouraged the collection and extensive planting of ferns and which saw that alpine plants were sufficiently popular for at least one firm to issue a catalogue entirely given over to them. Moreover, after the introduction of many Himalayan Rhododendrons by Joseph Hooker in 1850, the ensuing years were also notable for the vast number of hybrid rhododendrons raised by Waterer and by Standish and Noble.

Parks and places of public resort probably did overdo the bedding system, but it is unlikely that it had such a hold on the private gardener as the more gloomy horticultural writers would have us believe. The suggestion that, when the tide turned, nurserymen had to search for herbaceous plants from cottage gardens only proves that no one had troubled to read contemporary catalogues. The herbaceous plants were always available and so were presumably purchased in sufficient numbers to make their continued cultivation worthwhile.

The return to normality and the 'natural garden' were not long in coming, although the exotic bedders still had their parts to play in many gardens and, indeed, still do, even though they have tended to be replaced in most gardens by plants that may be called hardy bedders, chiefly the Hybrid Tea and Floribunda roses. It is not easy for us to conceive the immense brilliance and panache that the first beds of zonal pelargoniums and *Salvia spendens* must have contributed to the garden. Although by the mid-1840s the number of available plants had become very large, most of them had a comparatively short flowering period. It was possible to have a mass of scarlet by planting quantities of *Lychnis chalcedonica* – indeed this had been possible since the sixteenth century – but this mass would only last for two or three weeks at the most. But the fact that you could have a continuous display for months at a time must have been very exciting when it was novel.

Those of us who have indifferent taste are always rather liable to wish for a 'blaze' or a 'riot' of colour, and I suspect that the interest in alpines that arose around the 1860s was partly due to the realisation that when well-grown they produced a greater intensity of flower than any other subject. Writing in 1866, Robinson made great play of the fact that, 'Mr. Atkins . . . a gentleman with . . . a capital knowledge of alpine vegetation, has told me of having frequently spanned with his hand fifty flowers of one of these gentians fully opened at once on a plant not more than an inch high'. It would not be too much of an exaggeration to say that the alpine garden was, at first, the snobbish substitute for the bedding system which was becoming too plebeian. So if masses of flowers were to be seen, the alpine subjects presented the best means of producing such an effect. This is only one facet of the truth. After all, most alpine plants are very beautiful and, moreover, Switzerland was becoming a favourite holiday resort. In the *Floral World* for 1870 a Mrs. Webb gives directions for collecting plants in the Alps, packing them and re-establishing them on return. The development of the railway had made such expeditions far easier, as one could get from Switzerland to England in a couple of days, instead of taking a week as the old diligence had done, so that plants could be more easily transported successfully.

The bedding system was, in any case, dying of repetition. No longer was there the large choice which had formerly prevailed, and the parks had to ring changes on the old subjects. The taste for garish colours, which is always with us to a greater or lesser extent (as the success of the rose 'Super Star' shows) went into temporary abeyance. Robinson, who was always sensitive to the times, founded *The Garden* to combat the bedding system and inculcate the cultivation of hardy herbaceous subjects, as well as other plants. But, as might be expected, the first *rappel à l'ordre* came from Hibberd in his *Amateur's Flower Garden* of 1871. In his opening pages he states, 'Before flowers are thought of, a garden should be provided for the sustenance of a suitable extent of shrubbery, grass-turf, and other permanent features, to which the flowers will in due time serve for embellishment . . . A garden rich in trees and shrubs, with ample breadth of well-kept lawn, will be enjoyable at all seasons without the aid of flowers. A few simple borders, well stocked with mixed herbaceous plants, such as primulas, paeonies, lilies, phloxes, hollyhocks and carnations would, in many instances, afford more pleasure and ever-changing interest than the most gorgeous display of bedding plants hemmed in between two glaring walls, or exposed on a great tree-less, turfless place like the blazing fire at the mouth of a coal-pit. But given the good permanent substratum, the well-kept garden of greenery . . . then a brave display of flowers becomes the crown-ing feature. The argument may be summed up in this – that flowers alone do not constitute a garden; and when a garden has been provided to receive them, the display should be adapted in extent and character to the situation and its surroundings.'

This seems the most sheer common sense and scarcely a revolu-tionary statement, yet such it was. Later on, he again anticipates the Robinson school (for the sake of priorities we should perhaps say that Hibberd's book appeared in 1871, while Robinson's *The English Flower Garden* appeared in 1883) when writing about the herbaceous border. 'The hardy herbaceous border is the best feature of the flower-garden, though commonly regarded as the worst. When well-made, well stocked and well managed, it pre-sents us with flowers in abundance during ten months out of twelve . . . Given a few trees and shrubs, a plot of grass and comfortable walks, the three first essentials of a garden, a col-lection of hardy herbaceous plants is the fourth essential feature and may be the last . . . our business is to point out that the bedding system is an embellishment added to the garden: the herbaceous border is a necessary fundamental feature.' He would supplement the border with alpine flowers, 'a large number of which can be better grown and more thoroughly enjoyed in an airy and unheated greenhouse than when planted on the rockery in the open air'.

Hibberd seems to have been a pioneer in his advocacy of the alpine house, and though he returned to the subject from time to time (and even gave it its present name) there seems little evidence that this pioneer work was recognised at the time. This is by the way; the main point is that Hibberd re-proclaimed the essentials of a garden as being trees and shrubs, lawns, well-kept paths and a herbaceous border. He had been saying this since about 1860 with increasing emphasis. This attitude was reinforced by Robinson's journal *The Garden,* which started publication in 1872 – and with considerable vituperation – which would have defeated its object if the campaign had not already been won, by the same author's *The English Flower Garden,* which appeared in 1883.

A more significant publication of this writer was *The Wild Garden* (1871) which, in fact, if not in words, was a development of the wilderness of the seventeenth and eighteenth centuries. Here it was suggested that, in some part of the garden, plants should be inserted and then left as though they were native plants in their own haunts. Some of these suggestions were rather visionary. There is an illustration of myriads of peonies growing in grass. These must have looked superb when they were in flower, but, since it would have been impossible to cut the grass before the late autumn without killing the peonies, must have looked very untidy for the rest of the year. Nevertheless, the fact that some of his suggestions were impractical, does not interfere with his valuable idea that was to bear great fruit in the early parts of the present century.

The idea itself was not entirely new; there is a splendid description of a wilderness in Hibberd's *Rustic Adornments.* Although, here, he relies mainly on native wild flowers, when talking of ericas he does say that 'The ling and our own native ericas should mingle with some of the choicest of hardy heaths from the Cape, of which I would find at least thirty distinct kinds that would need no protection in winter'. What could these have been? In any case, the idea of devoting a single volume to the Wild Garden was Robinson's; like all his didactic books it is divided into two parts, the first detailing his arguments and the second a *catalogue raisonée* of suitable plants, some of which, such as *Polygonum cuspidatum,* experience has shown as dangerous when allowed into any part of the garden. Of all these specialised nineteenth-century gardens, the fernery seems to have fallen into at least temporary desuetude, but the rockery developed into the alpine garden and the wild garden into the woodland garden. Nothing else seems to have developed at all, but have remained much as they were in 1870; but although the designs have remained the same, the contents have altered and it is these we must now consider.

——9——
Into the Twentieth Century

HITHERTO, we have been considering the flower garden in terms of centuries, but, of course, gardeners do not wake up one day and say – 'Goodness me, it's 1900; we had better alter the garden'. Alterations usually come about because new materials are available. The most striking change in the twentieth century was the revelation of the great floral wealth of western China. Fortune and Maries had brought back many plants from eastern China. Maries had also, in the late 1870s, brought back a multitude of new plants from Japan, but these plants, though by no means insignificant, were as nothing to the flood which resulted from the expeditions of such men as E. H. Wilson, George Forrest and Frank Kingdon Ward, to name only the most famous. However, it is little use sending out plant collectors until you have some idea about what there is to collect. The knowledge of Chinese plants was mainly due to two French missionaries, Père David and Père Delavay and to an English customs official Augustine Henry. This took place between the mid-1870s to the 1890s, and a trickle had already started in France before the great abundance was received. Armand David himself sent back a number of plants and seeds, and some of Delavay's contemporaries, among whom Père Farges and Père Soulié are especially prominent, sent seeds to the firm of Vilmorin.

Indeed, one could make a claim that, in the late 1880s and early 1890s, France was for a short time the horticultural centre of the world. One cause was the work of M. Marliac-Latour, who suddenly astounded the gardening world by a number of hardy water-lily hybrids. Until this time, the number of interesting and showy aquatic plants had been somewhat limited. There were a number of plants considered suitable for fringing the edges of ponds or lakes, but very few, apart from the native *Nymphaea alba* and the brandy bottle, *Nuphar luteum*, were sufficiently hardy to grow outside. The N. American species, *Nymphaea tuberosa*, with flowers much like our own water-lily, but slightly larger and a far more vigorous plant and *N. odorata* were available early on, as was the very dwarf *N. pygmaea*, but they were all white-flowered. Towards the end of the 1870s, a reddish form of *Nymphaea alba* was discovered in Sweden and a pink form of *N. tuberosa* in the USA. Marliac-Latour used these coloured species as well, if his lecture to the RHS in August 1898 is to be trusted, as the tropical *N. rubra*. He also used the yellow-flowered *N. mexicana*, from the southern United States, in his hybrids. The results were a series of water-lilies with flowers ranging from deep crimson through the pinks to white and also yellow-flowered plants.

Water had always been a desired ingredient of a garden of any size. One of the most common criticisms of eighteenth-century gardens was that they lacked sufficient water, but it was regarded as an end in itself, either as a point of repose, where you could rest your eyes and enjoy the reflexions, or else as a cause of excitement in fountains and cascades. Water had hitherto been an essential part of the landscape garden, but had played no part in the flower garden. Marliac-Latour and his son-in-law Laydecker were to change all this. Many large gardens already had lakes or fountains, but water-lilies only need 18 ins. of water above their roots, so that many of the lakes were too deep. And they require the water to be still, so that ponds with fountains were unsuitable. Sometimes the old lakes were suitable; Brown's lake at Sheffield Park is now gay with crimson water-lilies, but often new ponds had to be created and in gardens of small size, where hitherto a pond was thought to occupy too much room, space had to be found to grow these fascinating new garden plants. A new phrase – 'the water garden' – thus came into existence. Slightly earlier, the introduction from Japan of *Iris ensata* (*kaempferi*) and *I. laevigata* had given added interest to the edges of streams and ponds. In reality, it would seem that the kaempferi irises are naturally plants of dry hillsides, but they seem to have responded well to these unnatural conditions and are still generally regarded as marsh plants. Apparently the confusion arose because the Japanese tended to flood the iris beds, when they were in bloom, in order to enhance the spectacle.

Another feature of the closing years of the nineteenth century and the opening years of the twentieth was the creation of pastiche gardens. The Japanese exhibition not only gave rise to the Mikado, it also led to a number of 'Japanese' gardens being built in English surroundings – sometimes, indeed, by gardeners especially brought over from Japan. These were usually built around a pool with, perhaps, a picturesque bridge, a stone lantern and maybe a bronze crane, while the planting would include *Wistaria* and *Acer palmatum* in various cvs. These features differed from the pagodas and Chinese summer houses of the eighteenth and nineteenth centuries in that they were not mere episodes, but a more extended piece of exotica. They doubtless gave great pleasure to their owners, but had no effect either on the use of flowers or of landscape design. Many still survive, but the largest, that at Friar Court, has gone and is chiefly remembered for its providing the occasion for a superlative display of tact. When he was shown it, the Japanese ambassador is said to have replied: 'Magnificent. We have nothing like it in Japan.'

Although so-called Italian gardens, characterised by terraces, fountains and statues had long been put into more pretentious acreages, the breeding of numerous handsome climbing roses, such as 'Crimson Rambler' (1893), 'Dorothy Perkins' (1901), 'Albéric Barbier' (1900) and 'American Pillar', together with the breeding of large-flowered Clematis from 1860 to 1880 caused the pergola to be much used in gardens in order to display these attractive flowers. This, in its ideal form, consists of an avenue of brick columns, with wooden crossbars, up and over which the climbers are trained. In Mediterranean climates it is used to give a cool, shady tunnel in the heat of the day, and has always looked a little strange in England. However, very little that is better has been invented to show off ornamental flowering climbers, and pillars, or wire pyramids are still used today for that purpose. The plants are, of course, also trained on walls and, occasionally, into trees and shrubs, but the idea of the pergola persisted up to

1939. Since then there has been a tendency for rose breeders to develop less vigorous climbers, while the breeding of Clematis seems practically to have ceased in 1880.

These fashions were somewhat transitory, but the rock garden has grown considerably both in size and in general interest. This is, of course, mainly due to the very large number of attractive plants that can be grown under these conditions, but the cult must also have been encouraged by the writings of Reginald Farrer (1880–1920). But, since his first book did not appear until 1907, there must already have been some considerable interest in the form and, indeed, as we shall see, a number of large rock gardens had already been built. Many of these were made by the firm of Backhouse, who, as we have seen, were already in the fore-front of the movement in the 1860s. In 1882, G. C. Joad of Wimbledon, who had specialised in rock plants and had even built a rock garden under glass, bequeathed his collection of over 2,500 alpine plants to Kew and the construction of the rock garden as a rocky valley was begun. In the 1890s came the rock garden of the great, but little-known gardener, Ellen Willmott, at Warley Place. This was made as a somewhat dramatic gorge. The rock garden at St. John's College, Oxford, which was a plantsman's paradise, was started in 1893. Large rock gardens were being erected all over the place, and the one at South Lodge, Lower Beeding, Sussex, still exists in an unspoiled condition.

The most famous of these, now alas gone for ever, was that built over a series of years by Frank Crisp (later given a baronetcy) at Friar Park, Henley. Contemporary writers always refer to him as 'jovial', and he seems to have had a rather prep-schoolish sense of humour, as had so many of the Edwardians. But he was no fool: he was learned, a successful expert in company law, and treasurer to the Linnaean Society. Henri Correvon, the great Swiss enthusiast for alpine gardening, spoke of his rock garden as the first in Europe, but it was, in some ways, rather strange. It was started at some time in the 1890s and was described in the *Gardeners' Chronicle* for October 28th 1899: 'This is no ordinary rock garden with a path down the centre and banks on either side; it is more like a model "Alps"; it stretches over a great space of ground, and there are represented in it, mountains of greater and lesser height, valleys, mountain passes . . . rustic alpine bridges overlooking quite formidable precipices, a waterfall etc. . . . The rockery has a range in height from 30 to 40 feet . . . It is made with good solid Yorkshire stones and over 2,000 tons have been brought to Friar Park from Leeds. One of these stones, that weighs 6½ tons, is a somewhat conspicuous object and in a rockery will remain such for some years.'

We learn that the oldest part was 'partly made by Backhouse', who also supplied many of the original plants, but later the Guildford Hardy Plant Co. was called upon 'to supply an immense number of plants, including all the choicest species this firm could furnish'. Sir Frank, however, did not rest on his laurels, and by 1909 the rock garden had been embellished by a scale model of the Matterhorn. The *Gardeners' Chronicle* recorded that 'the mountain top appears clothed in snow, the effect being obtained by the use of some alabaster. Appropriate plants are disposed at suitable spots, and the visitor can imagine himself to be in the midst of the Alps. Some idea of the extent of the rockery may be obtained from the fact that 7,000 tons of stone (from near Leeds) have been used in its construction, while it is furnished with 4,000 distinct plants.'

Later on, he embellished the scene still further with a small herd of cast-iron chamois. Still he was not satisfied. From this original rock garden you could descend into a series of caves and thence, later, you emerged into yet another rock garden, the shamrock garden: 'This . . . as its name implies, was wholly built of artificial rocks, so skilfully contrived that they might almost have taken in any but the trained geologist. They had begun as amorphous blocks of half-dried concrete, given stratification marks by scoring them with a piece of broken wood, brushed over with a stable brush to give them a striated and slightly roughened surface, dusted with sand and finished off with a spray of oxide of iron, or some such pigment. When set, they were ready for use, and had the advantage of being made of a shape and size to meet the needs of construction, rather than, as too often happens, making that depend upon the materials to hand. The finished product looked remarkably like a rock garden.' (*AGS Bulletin*, June, 1949.)

Such frivolous behaviour was anathema to Reginald Farrer, who wrote, 'Let your rock garden set out to be something definite, not a mere agglomeration of stones. Let it be a mountain gorge if you like, or the stony slope of a hill, or a rocky crest, or a peak. But, whatever it be, it must have definiteness of scheme. It is, in effect, an imitation of Nature, and, to be successful, must aim at reproducing with fidelity some particular feature of Nature – whichever you may choose.' (*The Rock Garden*, 1907.) He goes on to say that the Glen form, however essential it may have been at Kew, is apt to be monotonous, while the gorge at Warley was to his own taste 'a trifle too violent to be altogether pleasant'.

Farrer himself gardened at Ingleborough, where the surrounding landscape was fairly rocky, and he does not seem to have realised that in other landscapes, the sudden appearance of masses of rock – however artistically sited – is liable to appear somewhat incongruous, or that the appearance of glens, gorges, or hillocks in a predominantly flat area must be unconvincing. I suspect that Sir Frank, on the other hand, was well aware of this and, realising that the rock garden was an attractive and agreeable folly, deliberately accentuated its more amusing features, while still employing the best methods to grow the most attractive plants. The cast-iron chamois were the last straw for Farrer, who, when introducing a book by E. A. Bowles (*My Garden in Spring*, 1909) about his own garden at Myddleton House, spends much of his space in fulminating against Friar Park.

Be that as it may, it would certainly appear that it was Farrer's writings that encouraged the construction of large rock gardens in the gardens of the wealthy, and of small ones throughout the kingdom. The only trouble with these is that they can never be neglected for long without becoming invaded by coarse weeds and the more active of their occupants, which tend to smother the choicer plants. The 1914–18 War caused a certain reduction of these larger rock gardens, while after the 1939–45 War practically none survived in private hands, while those in public places, such as Kew and Wisley, had to be rebuilt and replanted. With a few exceptions we have to rely on photographs to appreciate the early alpine gardens. Nowadays the price of rocks is such that in most districts gardeners have reverted to Hibberd's and Robinson's idea of a raised bed, either with a dry walling elevation, or one consisting of peat blocks. Rocks in themselves, not being found necessary for the cultivation of most alpines, have tended to disappear from the garden, although every year an old-fashioned rockery appears at the Chelsea Flower Show.

Two inventions in this sphere are credited to Farrer – the moraine and the scree – both modifications adapted to the cultivation of high alpines requiring very rapidly draining soil. In both cases compartments in the rock garden are filled with a mixture mainly composed of limestone or granite chippings, with which a very small proportion of soil is mixed. In theory the moraine should be supplied with subterranean watering in the summer months, but this refinement was generally ignored, and the difference between the scree and the moraine garden is now mainly nominal. They work very efficiently for a few years, but then have to be renewed.

We have already seen how Joseph Hooker brought back a large collection of rhododendrons from his expedition to Sikkim, and a few further species were introduced a few years later by J. Booth. Some of these required greenhouse treatment and many were only hardy outdoors in selected districts. However, remembering the earlier successes when *R. arboreum* was hybridised with *R. catawbiense* and *R. caucasicum*, Waterer and Standish and Noble used these new introductions for further hybridising on these lines. The majority of the race now known as Hardy Hybrids was brought into being in the last three decades of the century. For example, 'Ascot Brilliant' appeared in 1861, 'Cynthia' in 1870, 'Pink Pearl' in the later 1890s, 'Sappho' about 1865 and 'Luscombei' in 1880.

Fortune's introduction of *R. fortunei* in 1855 proved a turning point in rhododendron hybridisation, as at last there was a reliably hardy parent that was neither *R. catawbiense* nor *R. ponticum* and which added fragrance to its other charms. I suppose the most famous of these crosses is 'Loderi' (1901). The other parent was a species that was to transform the hybrid race by adding great size to the individual flowers, namely *R. griffithianum*. This latter was one of Hooker's introductions, but was definitely tender and usually had to be grown in a greenhouse. In the 1880s (or possibly earlier) it was employed by the breeder J. H. Mangles and 'George Hardy' a cross between *R. griffithianu* pollinated by *R. catawbiense*, was one of the earliest large-flowered hybrids and it is, indeed, the pollen parent of the popular

'Pink Pearl'. At the same time the azalea section of the genus, which had been abundantly hybridised since the 1830s, was further increased by the introduction by Lobb from California of the late-flowering *R. occidentale*. The range of colours and the length of season was already quite remarkable, when, in the early years of the twentieth century, the first new species started to come in from China and the rhododendron scene was completely transformed. This, however, will be discussed in the next chapter.

Before going on to what I think is the most important aspect of flower gardening in the *fin-de-siècle* period, perhaps we had better recapitulate what the general attitude towards the flower garden had become. The shrubbery had been enriched, not only by introductions from Japan, but also by the new hybrid lilacs that Lemoine had bred in the 1870s. Using, it is said, the Chinese *Syringa oblata* (introduced to cultivation in 1856, although it is not clear by whom but possibly from the St Petersburg Botanic Garden, which sent many plants to Kew), he had obtained a large variety of colours in this favourite shrub, which hitherto had been either mauve or white; double-flowered forms also appeared. A number of new rose species were coming into cultivation, although they were only grown by 'curious gardeners'. On the other hand the development of the Hybrid Tea rose was being hurried along by M. Pernet-Ducher, who in 1883 began his attempt to breed the double 'Austrian Copper', *R. foetida* into the Hybrid Tea strain, although it was not until 1900 that his first success was commercially available.

In the herbaceous border both the delphinium and the bearded iris were being continually hybridised and large numbers of cvs were already available. These now seem rather small plants, since Sir Michael Foster introduced the tall tetraploid species as *I. trojana* – all of which arrived between 1880 and 1890 – although it was not until the early years of the twentieth century that their first progeny appeared. The lupin was also being hybridised. *L. polyphyllus* was the main plant used, although *L. arboreus* and *L. nootkatensis* were also bred into the strain, giving a certain amount of colour variant. Its most spectacular transformation, however, came much later. Daffodil breeding had been started in the early years of the nineteenth century by Dean Herbert, but it was only as the century advanced that it became a serious commercial undertaking, owing to the work of Peter Barr, Edward Leeds and William Backhouse (only distantly related to the famous nurseryman). By 1884, the number of named cvs was already enormous. In Barr's *Ye Narcissus* he lists as many as forty-five trumpet self-coloureds and twenty-eight bicolors. In addition, we learn from Backhouse in the *Gardener's Chronicle* for June 10th, 1865, that he crossed *Narcissus poeticus* × *pseudonarcissus* with *N. angustifolius* (whatever that may be, evidently a white-flowered species) and produced some green-flowered plants. The hybridists were also still busy with the gladiolus and the introduction of large-flowered species caused this plant, also, to have a much extended range of size and colour. The mixture was becoming too rich and someone had to try to organise this vast quantity of material that was now available to the gardener.

The designer who managed to put some sense of proportion and design into this plethora of floral wealth was Gertrude Jekyll (1843–1935). She was originally trained as a painter, but her bad sight made this difficult, and she started to design gardens, starting in the 1880s. It is not too easy to give an account of her principles, as each garden was considered as a problem to be considered on its own, but we may cite her insistence on space and proportion and the return to the principle of gradation of colours, which had been already propounded in the 50s, as we have seen, but which had been somewhat neglected in the search for brilliance of effect. Perhaps her greatest gift was a complete lack of prejudice. She could equally well design formal gardens to complement the houses of Sir Edwin Lutyens, with whom she constantly worked, or an informal garden when circumstances made that desirable. She was also associated with what she terms the gardens of special colouring and which some unsympathetic characters call outdoor upholstery, but she was never dogmatic about it.

'It is a curious thing that people will sometimes spoil some garden project for the sake of a word. For instance, a blue garden, for beauty's sake, may be hungering for a group of white lilies, or for something of palest lemon-yellow, but it is not allowed to have it because it is called a blue garden, and there must be no flowers in it but blue flowers. I can see no sense in this; it seems

20 The quintessential cottage garden
21 Littlecote – the principle of the cottage garden enlarged: the
    Robinsonian ideal

22 The calming influence of Gertrude Jekyll
23 The rock garden at Friar Park

to me like fetters foolishly self-imposed. Surely the business of
the blue garden is to be beautiful as well as blue. My own idea is
that it should be beautiful first, and then just as blue as may be
consistent with its best possible beauty. Moreover, any experi-
enced colourist knows that the blues will be more telling, more
purely blue, by the juxtaposition of rightly placed complementary colour.' (*Colour Schemes for the Flower Garden*, 1914.)

To prove her point, she supplies a plan for a blue garden, which
includes white everlasting peas, yuccas, a white tree lupin,
Thalictrum flavum, Lilium longiflorum and *L. suovitzianum,
Eulalia variegata*, variegated coltsfoot, pale yellow and white
snapdragons and a yellow *Verbascum* in addition to a large
number of blue plants. Similarly, her orange garden contains a
number of scarlet-flowered plants, while her grey garden contains
heliotrope, godetias, *Ageratum* and a number of white flowers.
No preconceived ideas are going to interfere with her overall
conception. Observing that there were few plants that had
imposing foliage in early spring, she firmly picked on one that
had, although later it would prove objectionable. This was the
burdock, which could easily, she assumed, be disposed of if it
attempted to flower. She did not believe in the school of thought
that puts a plant in and leaves it. Thus, of *Helianthus salicifolius*
she says, 'This is one of the perennial Sunflowers, that are usually
considered not good enough for careful gardening. It grows very
tall and bears a smallish bunch of yellow flowers at the top.' However, if the stems were gradually pulled horizontally, to cover
some earlier flowering plants, 'this pulling down, as in the case
of so many plants, causing it to throw up flower-stalks from the
axils of every pair of leaves; so that in September the whole
thing is a sheet of bloom'. Perhaps we may permit ourselves one
more quotation, depicting the arrangement of a herbaceous
border for June and July.

'The planting of the border is designed to show a distinct
scheme of colour arrangement. At the two ends there is a ground-
work of grey and glaucous foliage – Stachys, Santolina, Cineraria
maritima, Sea-Kale and Lyme-grass, with darker foliage, also of
grey quality, of Yucca, Clematis recta and Rue. With this, at the
near . . . end, there are flowers of pure blue, grey blue, white,
palest yellow and palest pink; each colour partly in distinct

masses and partly intergrouped. The colouring then passes
through stronger yellows to orange and red. By the time the
middle space of the border is reached the colour is strong and
gorgeous, but, as it is in good harmonies, it is never garish. Then
the colour recedes in an inverse sequence through orange and
deep yellow to pale yellow, white and palest pink; again with
blue-grey foliage. But at this . . . end, instead of the pure blues
we have purples and lilacs.

'Looked at from a little way forward . . . the whole border can
be seen as one picture, the cool colouring of the end enhancing
the brilliant warmth of the middle. Then, passing along the wide
path next the border . . . each portion now becomes a picture in
itself, and every one is of such colouring that it best prepares the
eye, in accordance with natural law, for what is to follow.'

There is, of course, a danger that this extremely artful arrangement of colours may appear too artificial and that the *ars celare
artem* may be conspicuously lacking; but, given the plethora of
colours that was available at the turn of the century, something
in this line was clearly called for. Moreover Miss Jekyll was no
fanatic, like her friend Robinson, who, when he purchased
Gravetye Manor, pulled all his greenhouses down. She, on the
other hand, had no objection to bedding plants: 'There has been
so strong a revulsion in garden practice since the days when the
bedding out of tender plants in stiff and not very intelligent ways
absorbed the entire horticultural energy of gardens that many
people have conceived a dislike for the plants themselves. It is a
common thing for friends to express surprise at seeing scarlet
Geraniums, yellow Calceolaria and blue Lobelia in my garden,
forgetting that it was not the fault of the plants that they were
misused or employed in dull or even stupid ways. There are no
better summer flowers than . . . Geraniums, and none so good for
such uses as the filling of tubs and vases.'

Much of Munstead Wood, her own garden, was divided into
separate compartments that could be viewed away from the rest
of the garden, so that there was the June garden, the July and
August garden, the spring garden and so on, which could be
neglected when not in their prime. This is not a type of gardening
that everyone can tolerate, as it sometimes induces a claustro-
phobic feeling and makes it difficult for anyone to appreciate the

overall design. Nevertheless, the idea has given rise to many admired gardens such as Sissinghurst and Hidecote and, of course, the principle of the small garden has been of inestimable value to small suburban gardeners, whose numbers have increased so markedly throughout the years.

We may well say that one aspect of the future was indicated by Miss Jekyll. Another aspect may have been foreshadowed by G. F. Wilson (1822–1902). In 1878 he purchased Oakwood, 'a farm of about 60 acres with an old oak wood'. Although it was not only the oak wood that Wilson used, it is important as the forerunner of the woodland garden that perforce had to be made when the Chinese and Tibetan rhododendrons started flooding in. Wilson planted the wood with rhododendrons and lilies, and many of them still survive, although now Oakwood is the Royal Horticultural Society's garden at Wisley. This was obviously an extension of the wilderness of the seventeenth and eighteenth centuries and of Robinson's wild garden, but with the emphasis mainly on shrubs and bulbs, although he grew kaempferi irises along his ditches.

The Early Twentieth Century

IN 1899, the firm of James Veitch and Sons, who had been sending collectors to various parts of the globe since the 1850s, sent E. H. Wilson out to western China, with obtaining seeds of *Davidia involucrata*, the handkerchief tree, as his main objective. This plant had been known as a herbarium specimen since 1870, when Armand David sent his collections from Yunnan back to Paris. In point of fact the plant was already – just – in cultivation; Père Farges had sent thirty-seven seeds to Vilmorin in 1897 though one only had germinated. Wilson had a nightmare journey. He was detained as a possible spy in French Indo-China for months, while, when he eventually reached China the Boxer Rising was at its height and murders of foreigners were a commonplace. Eventually he reached the town in Yunnan where Augustine Henry told him of the only place where he had seen the Davidia. When Wilson arrived there he found the tree had been cut down. It shows Wilson's determination in deciding to make the 1,000-mile journey which would bring him to *Davidia's* type locality, and there he was crowned with success. However, it was not only the *Davidia* that he sent back. He also returned seeds of no less than 976 species, besides a number of bulbous and rhizomatous plants.

Indeed, the mission was so successful that Veitch sent him out again in 1903, this time with instructions to go into the mountains to collect alpines, with his prime objective the monocarpic *Meconopsis integrifolia*. This trip was also successful, although Wilson's interests lay mainly in woody plants and in lilies.

Wilson was to make two further expeditions to China, in 1907
and in 1910, but then he would be working for the Arnold
Arboretum and Professor C. S. Sargent. Later, he was to visit
Japan, Formosa and Korea, but his Chinese expeditions revealed
more novelties than any other single collector can have produced.
The list is endless, or so it seems, with no less than fifty-six
rhododendrons, including such popular species as *RR. argyro-
phyllum, auriculatum, bureavii, concinnum, calophytum,
decorum, discolor, fargesii, insigne, oreodoxa, souliei, sutchuense*
and *williamsianum*. There were also, among other plants now
popular in gardens, at least nine acers; nine *Berberis* species;
Camellia cuspidata; *Clematis armandii*; five *Corylopsis* species;
five Deutzias; *Kolkwitzia amabulis*; *Magnolia delavayi* and *M.
wilsonii*; eight new lilies, of which *L. regale* is the most famous
and cost him a broken leg, and twelve Primula species, including
P. pulverulenta. The full list of his introductions is said to
number over 1,000.

Unfortunately in 1914 Sir Harry Veitch, who was then in
charge of the Veitch nursery, found that the lease of Coombe
Wood, where the Wilson plants were growing, was running out
and would not be renewed and, also, that there seemed no
members of the family willing to carry on after him, so the
business was wound up and the plants put up for auction. Many
of the larger woody plants had not reached maturity, so that the
more desirable ones had not been propagated. Even so, enough
had been received to transform the garden scene and to whet the
appetite of others.

Wilson's work was continued by George Forrest, who was first
sent to Yunnan in 1904 by a rich private collector A. K. Bulley,
a successful business man and wildly enthusiastic gardener, who,
quite incidentally, founded the nursery firm of Bees Ltd. Forrest's
first journey was even more nightmarish than Wilson's, and he
barely escaped with his life, but subsequently relations with the
Chinese became very equable and he was able to train a large
force of helpers in his collecting, so that plants could be marked
in flower, and his helpers be sent back in the right season. This
meant that very large quantities of seed were collected. Bulley
was chiefly interested in primulas and other alpines, so that the

majority of Forrest's later expeditions were financed by a syndicate headed by the Rhododendron Society, which was founded
in 1915. Not surprisingly, he was encouraged to concentrate on
that genus, and he was paid a bonus for each species new to
science that he introduced. Indeed, in the memorial volume to
him, published in 1952, he was credited with the discovery of 309
new species and the introduction of some 335 species altogether.
Although 309 species were founded on his sendings, this number
has now been reduced, as many were just variable forms of single
species. By no means all these species were generally hardy, and
not all were particularly ornamental, but they included such
plants as *R. griersonianum*, which is not only very ornamental in
itself, but has proved an outstanding parent for many scarlet-
flowered hybrids.

Besides rhododendrons, Forrest introduced most of the
popular Asiatic primulas, which are still in cultivation. In the
easy 'Candelabra' section, previous to Forrest's introductions,
only *P. japonica*, brought back by Veitch and by Fortune in 1860,
and *P. pulverulenta* brought back by Wilson from his 1903
expedition were available. Forrest was to add *PP. beesiana,
bulleyana, aurantiaca* and *helodoxa* from this section, all of
which are still in ample cultivation; he was also responsible for
introducing such popular, although less easy primulas, as *PP.
chionantha, sinopurpurea, viali (littoniana)* and *nutans*, while
his introduction of *P. malacoides* was an invaluable contribution
to the pot-plant trade, where, purely by means of selection, it has
been transformed.

There are innumerable other plants which owe their introduction to Forrest, from the attractive purple-coned *Abies delavayi*
var. *forrestii*, to a number of dwarf *Hemerocallis* species and
several *Nomocharis* species. Unfortunately, many of his introductions have proved somewhat tender. One should mention
Camellia saluensis, a delightful plant in itself, but possibly more
important as the parent of the 'Williamsii' hybrids, of which
C. japonica is the other parent, and the marvellous plant *Pieris
formosa forrestii*, with its racemes of lily-of-the-valley flowers and
its bright scarlet young growth, while the alpine gardener might
well give the palm to *Gentiana sino-ornata*, still the most reliable
prostrate, autumn-flowering gentian.

The third of these important collectors was Frank Kingdon Ward, who, again, was originally employed by A. K. Bulley and later set up as a freelance, financed by various syndicates. The place of his collecting was not so much China, as adjoining Tibet, North Burma and Assam, and he made, in all, twenty-three expeditions up to his death as recently as 1958. His explorations were usually solitary, or made with only a few non-botanical companions, so that most of his plants were selected personally. The result was that, although he may not have sent back so much seed as Forrest, the plants were usually of better forms. He also added greatly to the list of rhododendrons in cultivation, and he is fittingly commemorated by *R. wardii*, the hardiest and one of the best of the yellow-flowered species. Among his other introductions the most famous, perhaps, are the easiest and most popular of the blue poppies *Meconopsis betonicifolia* var. *baileyi* and the giant cowslip, *Primula florindae*, but there were few important genera that he did not augment from *Acer* to *Viburnum*.

Perhaps mention should also be made of the voyage of Purdom and Farrer to Kansu in 1914. Although this was mainly in search of alpine plants it also enriched our gardens with *Viburnum farreri (fragrans)*, which had previously been introduced by Purdom, but without attracting attention, *Buddleia alternifolia* and *Rosa farreri*, besides a large number of alpines.

Most of the results of these collectings, even the earliest ones of Wilson, remained relatively unknown until after 1918, so far as trees and shrubs were concerned. The herbaceous plants, naturally enough, became known sooner and the result was that, as far as the garden was concerned, certain genera became transformed. *Berberis*, for example, had scarcely been thought of as a berrying shrub before the *aggregata* series became known; *Sorbus*, which had formerly been a rather small genus, became a very large one, with fruits of white, pink and yellow as well as the well-known scarlet. Few plants are commoner today than the double pink Japanese cherries, but these only started to arrive at the start of the century. Delightful rose species such as *Rosa moyesii* and *R. hugonis* arrived, as well as the great climbers of synstylae *R.R. filipes, helanae* and *rubus*. (*R. brunonii* had already been known for a long time.) It must have seemed as though the choice of flowering shrubs available to gardeners had suddenly trebled.

Of all these huge importations, the one that has had most effect on gardens is the phenomenal increase in the number of *Rhododendron* species available. Now the rhododendron is a very variable plant, more so than the majority of flowering shrubs. For example, there is *R. pseudochrysanthum*, which is a rather drab little plant. But among the seedlings there arose one plant with very attractive, young growth and larger and more showy flowers, which was given an Award of Merit by the RHS. Now, if one wants to grow this plant, one can order the A.M. form, but it must be remembered that in order to obtain this a large number of seedlings had to be grown on to flowering stage. Rhododendron seeds are minute, but most species seem to germinate well, so that one might get many hundreds of plants from a pinch of seed, but until they flowered you had no idea as to whether they were good forms or not. As a result, those gardeners who subscribed to Forrest's or Kingdon Ward's expeditions found themselves with a very large number of seedlings – all, in theory, requiring to be grown on. Most rhododendrons grow in dappled shade, so that those with woods on their estates had them thinned and the interstices filled with these unknown seedlings. As they reached flowering stage, theoretically the bad forms would be culled and the good ones preserved although this did not always happen.

Thus arose the rhododendron wood, which is the twentieth-century's most obvious contribution to garden design. Perhaps one would do better to call it a woodland garden, as other plants, *Sorbus, Malus, Prunus, Meliosma* etc. could also be grown under these conditions. It is an apotheosis of the wilderness and American gardens of the eighteenth and nineteenth centuries, but it is, of course, only possible for reasonably large estates. Unfortunately its effective life, if not kept regularly in good condition, is somewhat limited and some of these woodland gardens have now become enormous 'Victorian Shrubberies', requiring bulldozers and ample labour to bring them back to a condition in which it is possible to walk among the trees and shrubs, and to see which plants are worth preserving and which should be thrown out. This condition has been caused mainly by economic difficulties, resulting in curtailment of gardening staff, and in the fact that such gardens had to remain untended, or virtually so, between 1939 and 1945. There is no reason why, if constant attention can be given, the woodland garden should not remain in being for the length of life of its components. There are some rhododendrons that are known to be a century old, but what the general figure can be will probably be found to vary according to the size of plant and the time it takes to reach flowering size. For example, most of the 'Taliense' series have seemed to take many years to attain flowering dimensions – so that it might be presumed that they will prove long-lived – while species that come into flower in four or five years from seed may be proportionately shorter lived. The majority have been so short a time in cultivation that this vital figure can only be guessed at.

The majority of the new Sino–Himalayan rhododendrons have proved to be hardy in most parts of the British Isles, and have been extensively interhybridised, so that the number of species and hybrids available to anyone with an acid soil is now enormous. It is generally accepted among rhododendrophils that the true species have more grace and character than the hybrids, but, on the other hand, the hybrids are generally more floriferous and may well be stronger growers owing to 'heterosis', the phenomenon known as hybrid vigour.

A somewhat unexpected result of the importation of wild plants from China and Japan has been the creation of a vast number of hybrid *Hemerocallis* types, which might be termed the glory of the hybridist. The actual species are not among the most attractive of herbaceous plants, although they have a rather restrained charm, but the hybrids have an extended range of colours through palest yellow to maroon and a variety of habit from dwarf to three feet high. Moreover, the hybridists seem to have avoided the fatal trap of size that always seems to lure plant breeders from what one would imagine should be the true aim of an acceptable plant with leaves and flowers in proper proportion. Thus at one time we had dahlias such as 'Crawley Beauty' with flowers over a foot in diameter, roses so large that the centre was liable to start rotting before the flower opened properly and the great mop-headed 'Japanese' chrysanthemums. Fortunately, *Hemerocallis* seems to have no equivalent of *Hippeastrum leopoldii,* so that the flowers have remained of a decent size. Since the plants are thrifty, very hardy and increase fairly rapidly, we might well consider the new *Hemerocallis* types as the most valuable contribution to gardening of the century. Its main practitioners were Dr. A. B. Stout of New York and Messrs. Yeld and Amos Perry in Great Britain. They, at least, were the pioneers.

The science of genetics is of this century, and although its application to plant breeding has been mainly confined to food crops, some of its principles have naturally been applied by those working among the flowers. However, the most significant results have only been seen comparatively recently and will be briefly indicated in the next chapter.

Apart from the new woodland gardens, the English flower garden did not much alter in layout from what it had been in the *fin-de-siècle* period, although the contents of the various departments, herbaceous, alpine, marsh and shrubby were considerably increased. The herbaceous border was much enriched by the development of the tall bearded iris, which used the tetraploid species introduced by Michael Foster as parents, so that the resultant plants were considerably taller than those of the old 'Pallida-variegata' hybrids. Second and third generation hybrids also greatly extended the colour range, so that pinks and reds entered into the irises. Attempts to breed in the spectacular but recalcitrant Oncocyclus irises, were occasionally successful. but with less gratifying results than might have been expected. Hybridisation also took place between the various dwarf bearded irises and between these and the tall bearded to give a race known as Median irises.

Apart from the *Hemerocallis,* the most spectacular addition to the herbaceous border was the breeding of the 'Russell' lupins. George Russell started breeding lupins in 1911, apparently by obtaining as many species as possible and leaving it to nature to interbreed them, sowing the seed and then indulging in rigorous selection. It was not until 1937 that the results were commercially available, but the singular extension of the colours of *L. polyphyllus* (which had formerly been, bluish, white, pale yellow, pale pink with the occasional bicolor) to deep crimson, bright yellow, orange and various combinations, meant that the herbaceous border could be much more brilliant early in its career. Delphiniums became extremely tall, with huge florets, and were a clear example of the deceptive lure of excessive size. In 1924, the Danish breeder Poulsen introduced a new race of roses with moderately large flowers produced in clusters. This was to lead to the new breed of Floribunda roses.

The great advantage of the alpine garden is that a very large number of plants can be grown in a restricted space, so that people with very modest plots could grow a much greater variety in this section than in either the herbaceous or the ligneous. And the number of alpine plants available – the description was applied to all low-growing plants, not necessarily montane, thyme, for example, could be reckoned an alpine – increased to a prodigious degree between 1900 and 1939, many skilled nurserymen specialising entirely in these plants. Their attraction may have been increased by the charm of some of the writers on the subject; we have already mentioned Farrer and, in different style, the writings of Clarence Elliot must also have encouraged many to indulge in this style of gardening. Although the megalithic rock gardens of the late years of the nineteenth and early years of the twentieth century were still, occasionally, erected, it was the small rock garden that dominated the 1920s and '30s.

The war of 1914–18 caused the disappearance of many of the ranges of greenhouses, regarded as so essential to the well-to-do before that time, but the actual design of the garden only changed slightly after the holocaust. Except for public authorities, most bedding plants of the nineteenth century gave way gracefully to the Hybrid Tea rose, while the increased abundance of ornamental trees and shrubs meant that most large landowners increasing their plantings went in for these subjects, not so much because they entailed less work, as in the early stages this is barely true, but because their plantings could be left without renewal for many years.

═══ I I ═══

Up to the Present

THE WAR OF 1939–45 had a far more devastating effect on gardens than that of 1914–18. As much land as possible was turned over to the production of food, so that nurserymen had to sacrifice their stocks, usually by two-thirds; greenhouses were also called into the need to produce food and this generally meant that practically all the ornamental plants had to be sacrificed. Gardening staff were either absorbed into the armed forces or redirected into agricultural work. During these six years, weeds invaded the flower gardens, while the woodland gardens became overgrown with brambles and nettles and the stronger plants flourished at the expense of the smaller and weaker. Lawns were ploughed up and trees were cut down.

When peace returned, the first requirement of many gardens, particularly those of any size, was reclamation. This was aided, in some degree, by the agricultural chemists who produced a variety of herbicides, so that it was possible to destroy the nettles and brambles, although this could not always be done without sacrificing the ornamentals. Many moderately-sized gardens had been kept going by the devoted labour of elderly folk, who were considered not to have enough stamina to assist the war effort, but many other gardens practically disappeared – only established trees persisting without much damage. Shrubs untended grew thickly together, and the garden scene, when peace returned, was generally depressing. Moreover, gardening staff were very hard to obtain. The vast amount of reconstruction required in all forms of industry, and the clearing and rebuilding of bombed areas, offered work which was less laborious and better paid than that of the gardener; the fact that it was much less interesting only became apparent later, and, in any case the greater financial reward was liable to appear more attractive. Thus many large gardens, which had formerly given employment to forty men, considered themselves lucky if they had six, while for the smaller garden it was either a case of 'do-it-yourself' or relying on some-one who could give you two days a week.

The result of this was various suggestions for labour-saving gardens. Shrubs, although they took longer than herbaceous plants to come to flowering size, were thought to require less maintenance and the first casualty of the post-war years was the herbaceous border, which had been the lynch-pin of the Jekyll–Robinson school. It could be, and was, argued that it lacked interest before mid-June, while shrubs could produce flowers from the *Hamamelis* in January onwards, although this argu-ment omitted to point out that the number of shrubs that bloom after July is restricted, that most of these are white-flowered and thus there becomes a gap in the shrub garden between mid-July and October when ornamental fruits ripen and the autumnal tints start. It was also found that while the shrubs were small the interstices were liable to fill with noxious weeds whose removal required as much labour as the despised herbaceous border. This led to the recommendation of ground-cover plants – these were plants that would grow rapidly, so that they, in turn, smothered the weeds, but that were ornamental and would remain low-growing and not smother the developing shrubs. In fact, they were really a selection of ornamental weeds and we may live to regret their present popularity as we already regret the intro-duction of the bronze-leaved *Oxalis corniculata* in the late 1850s and the pink *Oxalis floribunda*.

One of the most time-consuming and laborious departments of the garden is the lawn and in many small town gardens it has disappeared to make way for the paved patio, but most people seem determined to preserve the lawn, in spite of the labour involved, and it is, of course, the ideal place for the children to play without committing excessive mayhem among the orna-mentals. Thus the lawn persists despite its obvious disadvantages. Throughout the last 100 years, attempts have been made to find a substitute for grass that would entail less labour in the way of mowing and general upkeep, but neither the *Sagina* of the late 1850s, nor the present-day chamomile, seem to have the advantages claimed by those who promulgated the ideas originally. Paving is an obvious solution where fairly small areas are concerned, but it entails considerable capital outlay, although the later maintenance is very small, while the lawn is comparatively cheap to lay, but requires continual maintenance.

Here again, the engineers have helped. The machine powered by a small petrol engine, although easier to manipulate than the hand-pushed one, seemed to entail a lot of time and temper in getting the engine to start and continue in good running order; the introduction of the mowing machine with an electric motor made this particular chore considerably easier, although one has to take care not to mow one's lead as well as the grass. Indeed, electric power has made many of the more laborious garden chores much simpler. Electric hedge trimmers mean one can keep one's hedge tidy much more rapidly, and with a smaller expenditure of energy. The electric greenhouse, although very costly if every gadget is installed, can be automated to the extent that very little work at all is needed, so long as there is no interference with the power supply. It can be automatically heated, ventilated and even watered. The thermostatically-controlled electric heater is admirable for the small greenhouse, although for larger structures, the circulation of hot water still appears more economic. However, the boilers now tend to burn oil rather than solid fuel, so that the laborious work of stoking and clinkering is now a thing of the past.

Petrol or diesel-driven miniature tractors, which will plough, harrow and hoe, are admirable in the vegetable garden, but only of use in the flower garden when you are creating new beds or borders. Otherwise, between your plants you must either rely on hand weeding and hoeing, or use some of the new herbicides, which are non-persistent, such as paraquat. These must be used with care, as they are not selective and will kill any plant with which they come in contact – in the case of irises they seem to be taken up by the roots and a wide berth must be given when applying herbicides round these subjects. Insect and fungus pests can now be controlled by systemic insecticides and fungicides, which are absorbed by the plant and remain active for many days. Unfortunately, the systemic insecticides are quite lethally poisonous and must be used with care, wearing goggles and protective clothing. And, of course, they must be kept well out of the reach of children. The chemists and the engineers have made gardening easier, so that one man can now cope with a larger area than he could formerly have done.

Although, with all the Chinese importations coming into flower, the interest of the shrub garden was enormously increased, it was not quite as trouble-free nor so continuously interesting as its proponents had suggested, and herbaceous plants started to make a come-back. However, it was generally accepted that the long, wide, old herbaceous border, magnificent though it may have been in its greatest presentations, as, for instance, at Hampton Court, was far too elaborate for most gardens and required far too much labour. It was therefore cut into sections and herbaceous beds – called Island Beds by their populariser Alan Bloom – reappeared. These, as we have seen, had already been used by Loudon's contemporaries and so, like so many so-called gardening novelties, they were simply a return to earlier practices. There was little difference in the species used in the herbaceous department, but some of the hybrids had, perforce, to undergo a change. Delphiniums growing to a height of 7 ft., of which 2 ft. were solid flowers, were extremely impressive. But they would not remain upright without support and the modern gardener does not want to waste his time and money purchasing stakes and tying plants to them. Rather, he prefers a smaller delphinium that will remain erect without support. The same happens with other herbaceous plants – gladioli, dahlias, Michaelmas daisies and the like.

Apart from having to produce plants of moderate size, and despite the increasing knowledge of genetics, the products of the hybridist since 1945 are not particularly impressive. An exception must be made, although they still await commercial release, for the Delphinium University Hybrids, bred by Dr. Legro, between the blue *elatum* strain and the scarlet *D. nudicaule* and the yellow *D. zalil*, to give plants with flowers the size of *elatum*, but with scarlet and yellow colours. The Poulsen roses have turned into the race known as Floribunda, in which the emphasis is much more on the rose as a bedding plant, and large numbers of flowers are a first requisite. Also, it may be noted with relief, the flowers are smaller and so in proportion to the size of the bush. Shortly after the war the Hybrid Tea roses – particularly those bred by M. Meilland of which 'Peace' is probably the most famous – became ridiculously large in size. 'Peace', with a flower up to 6 ins. across, might be acceptable as a cut flower, but growing on a bush less than 2 ft. high it appeared disproportionate. The trouble was that the Hybrid Tea swayed between being a bedding plant and a cut flower, so that it was never really wholly satisfactory in either category. Later bred roses in this class have smaller flowers that appear better suited to the size of the plant. On the other hand, the colour range has been extended. The scarlet pigment pelargonidin first made its appearance in the rose known as 'Superstar', while a number of greyish violets have also appeared, although this colour had been foreshadowed in such nineteenth-century roses as 'Reine des violettes'.

A striking feature of the post-war years has been the revival of the old shrub roses, some dating back to Tudor times, but most from the early nineteenth century. Although these only flower once a year, they have fragrance and a grace of form which most of the Hyrid Teas lack. The influence of *Rosa gigantea* in the Hybrid Tea strain gave a flower that looked exquisite when only partially opened, but which was liable to turn into a shapeless blob when fully expanded. This interest in roses before the introduction of *R. chinensis* was started before the war by such pioneers as E. Bunyard and V. Sackville-West, but it remained a rather esoteric cult until after 1945. Looked at as dispassionately as possible, most of these roses have rather muddy colours of pink, crimson and purple, but they are extremely attractive in form when fully open and generally have an exquisite fragrance. And it is interesting to note that some contemporary breeders are employing them with the Hybrid Tea strain in an attempt to produce a compact bush with the clearer colours of the Hybrid Teas, but with the attractive quartered centres of the Gallicas and Bourbons.

The interest in features other than flowers, to which we will come shortly, has also increased the interest in the species and

24 Development of Victorian bedding into the rose garden
25 A bog-and-stream garden

26 The woodland garden

hybrids therefrom, that have attractive heps or attractive foliage, or, in the case of *R. sericea*, 'Pteracantha', attractive thorns. Thus we find increasing use of roses such as *R. moyesii* and its hybrids, which, in spite of a singularly graceless habit, have large crimson flowers and even more conspicuous scarlet flask-shaped heps up to 6 ins. long in the autumn. *R. rubrifolia* has somewhat inconspicuous flowers and heps, but is much grown on account of its attractive mauvy-grey foliage; the white-flowered form is somewhat more attractive so far as floral display is concerned. The fact that some roses have only a short season of flowering has not militated against their being further hybridised, and the splendid plants created by Herr Kordes by crossing *R. spinosissima* with a very vigorous Hybrid Tea 'Joanna Hill' – of which 'Fruhlingsgold' is most often seen and which was the earliest to be released (1937) – are outstanding. The even more spectacular 'Fruhlingsmorgen' (1941) has a slightly different parentage, although *R. spinosissima* is still present as one parent.

Another aspect of roses deserves passing notice as being a post-war creation. These are the rather moderate climbers known as 'Pillar Roses', which, unlike the majority of climbing roses, tend to have a fairly extended season of flowering, but which are by no means easy to accommodate in most gardens, as 8 to 10 ft. is usually the extent of their height. However, such plants as 'Danse du feu' (1953), 'Golden Showers' (1956) and 'Parade' (1953) all have the habit of almost continual flowering, so it is worth making some effort to try to accommodate them somewhere in the garden. The trouble is they do not appear to be true climbers, such as can support themselves if trained through trees or shrubs, but need some support to keep them erect.

The arrangement of cut flowers was a great inspiration to many seventeenth-century Dutch painters, but we do not hear of its being taken seriously in England before the late 1860s and early 1870s, when the Misses March designed the Marchian Tazza, in which flowers were to be arranged. The first professional flower arranger (so far as I know), Miss Annie Hassard of St. Ronan's, Upper Norwood, started writing in the *Floral World* in 1872 and later collected her various articles into an instructive book. After 1945, thanks mainly to the remarkable work of the late Miss Constance Spry, considerably increased interest was taken in flower arrangement, with the result that many flowers not previously much cultivated in gardens have now become popular, not only for their use in these floral decorations, but also for their purely garden value. Gertrude Jekyll's most significant remark, 'Green is also a colour', was made to emphasise the importance of foliage in garden design, but it has now been adapted to include an interest in greenish flowers, with the resultant popularity of various Euphorbias, hitherto little grown, and plants such as *Veratrum album*, various hellebores and other similar plants.

Related to this is the increased interest in plants with ornamental foliage. Very large leaves had been regarded as subtropical in the 1870s, and plants such as *Macleaya (Bocconia)* and the giant sea kale *Crambe cordifolia* had been grown as much for their foliage as for their flowers and the various hostas were extensively used by Gertrude Jekyll (who, prophetically, also recommended *Euphorbia veneta (wulfenii)*), but it was the greenhouse that was the main centre of interest in foliage plants, where such brilliant leaves as provided by the various dracaenas, caladiums, codiaeums, rex begonias and calatheas were all widely cultivated.

As a result of both the wars, the big greenhouse nurseries went out of existence and stocks of many plants were only preserved in a few botanic gardens. Orchids were still largely cultivated, but many other greenhouse plants were lost, it would seem, for ever. In the last century many nurserymen, but Veitch in particular, had bred a race of so-called Javanicum rhododendrons which could be had in flower at any period in the year, with the help of a warm greenhouse. These have now almost entirely disappeared. However, a resurgence of interest in greenhouse foliage plants was at hand from an unexpected source. Perhaps the most pronounced feature of post-war years has been increasing urbanisation and the scarcity of land. More and more people are forced in live in flats, while even those who purchase a newly-built house find only a minute garden with it.

Oddly enough it seems to be a necessity for most people to have some living plants in their immediate vicinity, so, lacking a garden, they brought plants into the house and a large greenhouse industry producing 'house plants' came into being. Central heating became more widespread, so that the range of plants that could be grown in the home became considerably extended, although it was mainly restricted to those that did not require too brilliant a light, as that is not easy to supply in any house. In this connection, it is interesting to note that some modern houses are indulging in sun rooms, virtually an adaptation of the Victorian conservatory, in order to be able to grow more plants. But for those who have to put up with subdued light, foliage plants are more suitable than plants with brilliant flowers. Also, since they are to be looked at for 365 days in the year, it is preferable to have some plant that is always attractive, like a *Calathea*, to one that, like the Indian azalea, may be brilliant for two weeks, but is of little interest for the remaining fifty.

This interest in foliage spread from the house into the garden and not only was there increased interest in variegated sorts of normally green-leaved plants, but also in those with grey or silver foliage, as well as the graceful, fern-like leaves that had always been admired. This tendency was particularly noted among shrubs and trees, while other attributes (which had already been considerably studied at the start of the century when such gardens as Sheffield Park and the Westonbirt Arboretum were being planted) such as autumn leaf colour and colourful fruits were also recognised as being of nearly equal importance to the floral display. This has led to a change in the aspect of the shrub garden, where such old favourites as *Lilac* and *Prunus serrulata* are less planted than formerly, to give place to plants such as the various *Malus* and *Sorbus* species and hybrids, while plants such as *Eleagnus* are coming more and more to the fore.

The multiplicity of interests that can be found in trees and shrubs is much rarer in herbaceous and bulbous subjects, and these are still mainly grown for their floral display alone, with a few notable exceptions such as *Actaea* and *Iris foetidissima*, where the fruits are the main reason for their presence. One or two exceptional plants, like most of the hardy cyclamen, combine attractive flowers with attractive leaves, but these tend to be the exception. However, there is a noticeable return to the fashion of the 1870s for ornamental grasses, and there are a number of herbaceous plants grown principally for their foliage, most notably *Hosta*, artichokes and *Veratrum*. The principles of Miss

Jekyll are still very much with all garden designers. The choice
of plants, however, is very much less. Shrubs appear to have been
fairly well preserved, but if you compare a herbaceous or an
alpine catalogue of 1936 with one of 1970 you will find that the
choice is considerably smaller, although, it must be admitted,
has increased quite notably in the last few years.

There have been a certain number of new plants introduced
from expeditions to Turkey, Iran and Afghanistan, although we
have yet to see any that look as though they will become garden
favourites. The primulaceous genus *Dionysia*, barely in cultivation before 1939, is being raised in many alpine houses, while
other are wrestling with the beautiful, but very difficult, Juno and
Oncocylus irises, many of which are re-introductions, but some of
which are new to cultivation. As I write there has been an expedition to collect plants in the Andes, but whether any of the
marvellous plants that grow there will prove suitable for gardens,
as opposed to frames and alpine houses, remains a moot point at
the moment.

The hybridists appear to have gone on breeding the same
plants that have been popular for so long. A race of remontant
bearded irises that flower in early summer and again in autumn
sound promising, but seem to depend too much on a hot dry
summer to be very reliable. Otherwise, they seem to lack enter-
prise. For example Messrs. Ludlow and Sherriff introduced from
Tibet a very large vigorous shrub to which the name *Paeonia
lutea*, var. *ludlowii* has been given. When the ordinary *Paeonia
lutea* was crossed with the tree paeony, *P. suffruticosa*, some
unusual hybrids were produced (but all, so far as I know, before
1914). Why, one asks, has no one crossed the vigorous Ludlow
plant with *P. suffruticosa*, which might give rise to a genuine
tree paeony, as opposed to the rather low bush that exists at the
moment? As it is, if a gardener of 1873 was transported to our
modern garden, he might find improved cvs, but the only real
novelty would be the hybrid *Hemerocallis*. The gardener from
1773 would find many novelties, but he would look in vain for
any named *Ranunculus* species, would find only a handful of
English and Spanish irises and practically no double hyacinths.

It would appear, indeed, as though the outlook for the garden
were not too bright. Most modern houses have very little garden

space attached, while the large estates, when they change hands or when they come under the beneficient guardianship of the National Trust, tend to be kept as they were, with only a few embellishments. Often this is just as well; we do not really want the old masterpieces of garden design and old well-considered plantings altered, but it would be nice to think that the modern designer had some scope outside Brazil. Not that anyone seems to have any revolutionary ideas in design and, quite possibly, none are possible. One can feel fairly sure that the English flower garden will persist, as long as the atmosphere remains sufficiently unpolluted, but, at the moment, it does look as though it will consist of further variations on the old theme, using further variations on the old flowers. Still the number of possible variations must still be large, so perhaps we should not despair. The flower garden has given enormous pleasure and caused no harm for many years: it is not of many human creations one can say as much.

Postscript

In Mawe and Abercrombie's *The Universal Gardener and Botanist* there is a description of the flower garden in the late eighteenth century. This quotation is taken from the second edition, published in 1797, but may be taken as dating from somewhat earlier:

'A commodious space for a flower-ground, distinct from the other divisions . . . is most necessary for the culture of the more curious and valuable kinds of flowers.

'This principal flower-ground forming a distinct division, exclusive of other flower compartments distributed in different parts in contrast with the shrubbery clumps, etc., should be allotted for a choice collection of the finest kinds of both bulbous and fibrous-rooted flowers. The form of this ground may be either square, oblong, or somewhat circular; having the boundary of the division formed by an arrangement of a curious shrubbery, embellished with a collection of the most beautiful flowering shrubs; and the interior part should be divided into many narrow compartments, either in the manner of a parterre, formed into straight borders, beds, etc., edged with box, or divided into plain four-feet wide beds arranging parallel, having two-feet wide alleys between bed and bed; in either method having a walk carried all round next the outer boundary, then a border surrounding the whole division, and within this have the various division of beds, etc., as above, raising them generally in a gently rounding manner, highest in the middle, and edge the compartments principally with dwarf box, and some with thrift and pinks by way of variety, laying the walks and alleys with the finest gravel.

'In this division you may deposit the finest hyacinths, tulips, polyanthos-narcissus, jonquils, ranunculus, anemones, and all the other more curious, hardy bulbous and tuberous rooted flowers; each sort principally in separate compartments, especially of the choicer kinds; which being necessary both for distinction's sake and for the convenience of giving them occasional protection from inclement weather...

'Likewise in this division should be planted a curious collection of the finest fibrous-rooted flowery plants, as carnations, polyanthuses, auriculas, and many other curious sorts, arranging some of the most valuable in beds separately: others may be dispersed in different compartments, forming an assemblage of various sorts.

'In other compartments may exhibit a variety of all sorts, both bulbous and fibrous rooted kinds.'

I must also include another quotation from the same article, which seems to contradict, in part, what happened with the rock-garden:

'Likewise in some parts is exhibited artificial rock-work, sometimes contiguous to some grotto, fountain, rural piece of water etc., and planted with a variety of saxatile plants, or such as grow naturally on rocks and mountains.'

It does look as though the alpine garden was somewhat earlier in conception than had been imagined.

Bibliography

I have not listed here works quoted in the text where references are given.

Allan, Mea, *The Tradescants*, 1964
Birrell, F., ed., *Diary of a Scotch Gardener at the French Court*, 1931
Brett-James, N., *Life of Peter Collinson*, 1926
Darlington, W., *Memorials of John Bartram and Humphrey Marshall*, 1849
Dillwyn, L. W., *Hortus Collinsonianus*, 1843
Fox, R. Hinston, *Dr John Fothergill and His Friends*, 1919
Hadfield, M., *Gardening in Britain*, 1961
Lemmon, K., *The Covered Garden*, 1962
Taylor, G., *Victorian Flower Garden*, 1952
—, *Some Nineteenth Century Gardeners*, 1951

Much of the information about plant introductions come from my own unpublished researches into the subject.

Index